The Solution Oriented Mind

Dr. J. M. Bonard

Published by Palm Beach Editorial Services

West Palm Beach FL 33405

United States of America

ISBN 978-0-9831530-5-4

Library of Congress Control Number 2014956572

Layout by DidotGraphicDesign.com

Cover Illustrations by Joonas Isotalo

Copyright© 2015 Dr. J. M. Bonard

All rights reserved, which includes the right to reproduce this book or portions thereof in any form whatsoever except as provided by the U.S. Copyright law.

Printed in the United States of America

Foreword:
A Book That Will Enlighten and Uplift

By Michel Lamartine Porcena, Ed.D

I accepted without hesitation and with great pleasure the request to write a foreword note for *The Solution Oriented Mind*, an interesting book written by my colleague and friend, Dr. J.M. Bonard. I always knew him as a good husband, a concerned father, a dynamic and esteemed preacher with his own style, and a gifted and strong leader. But, I discovered through his book that more than all that, he is also a motivational writer. I am delighted to recommend *The Solution Oriented Mind*, a work that will inspire and motivate you to learn how to live a more rewarding and successful life.

From my own perspective, the book is a real challenge – the challenge to live a life of excellence and to fulfill our God-given destiny. I must admit that what I found in Dr. Bonard's book is far beyond what I could have imagined.

It is a known fact that as human beings, we have tremendous potential. Most people want to live life to the fullest. This book will encourage you to reach your unique God-given potential, to become all that God has created you to be by helping you uncover your hidden resources. *The Solution Oriented Mind* is a motivational book on how to succeed, not only according to man's criteria, but according to God. It is a refreshing, straightforward and balanced approach from a Christian perspective.

With the combined weight of his solid education and years of experiences as a pastor to support him, it is not surprising that Dr. Bonard would produce a motivational book of such significance as this one. But, most importantly, it is a book for people who need positive changes in their journey, people who want success in this world and in the world to come. Within these pages, the author addresses various topics such as: *Flying Above Life's Challenges, Turning Life's Setbacks into A Ladder to Success, Getting Rid Of Fear, Change from Sunset Mentality to Sunrise Mentality,* and *Plugging Into Life's Energy Outlet.*

The text is replete with illustrations drawn from nature that make the reading enjoyable and will enlighten and uplift you. The quality of the book will speak for itself. Dr. Bonard draws on the vast experience he's gained from his own spiritual journey to inspire others in the pursuit of progress and to argue on behalf of the endless possibilities of the human mind. His invitation to all those who are serious about spiritual development is wise, informed, lucid and utterly persuasive.

His purpose is to draw our attention to the power that is readily available to us when we become solution oriented. With candor, clarity and passion, the author provides insight into the endless possibilities God has placed before us. In reading this book, you will discover that one of the key elements to achieving success in life is to program your mind to make it a solution oriented mind.

The Solution Oriented Mind is a rare treasure, inspired by the Spirit and born of practical experiences. This book is so articulate that no reader can come away without a fresh perspective on how to improve one's life. I cannot think of anyone who wouldn't be helped by reading it. More than that, every Christian should embrace its principles.

Dr. Bonard's insights make me wish I could begin my Christian journey all over again. It made me exclaim: Here is another book that every Christian should read. At any rate, I invite you to follow him in his remarkable common sense approach. Read carefully, thoughtfully, and intentionally to understand its principles and to put them into practice. You will be happy you did.

- Kissimmee, FL, November 5, 2014

Acknowledgements

I owe much to my wife, Regine, who supports me with patience, understanding, and great devotion. Words alone cannot express how much I love and appreciate her for demonstrating such great qualities. I also owe much to my three sons, Bonard, Jr., Jonathan and Jeremy, for believing in me.

I particularly want to thank Dr. Michel Lamartine Porcena, a committed university president and gifted leader whose integrity, spirituality, and successful ministry have always influenced me in my own spiritual journey.

I want to express my thanks to John Nelander of Palm Beach Editorial Services and Hanna Isotalo, graphic designer, who devoted quality time in editing the final copy of *The Solution Oriented Mind*.

My most profound gratitude goes to Jesus Christ, the inspiration and guiding hand for *The Solution Oriented Mind*.

Table of Contents

Introduction: Explore the Possibilities of the Human Mind 10

Chapter 1: Flying Above Life's Challenges 13

Chapter 2: Turning Life's Setbacks into a Ladder to Success 37

Chapter 3: Getting Rid of Fear 53

Chapter 4: Restoring Life's Vessel 71

Chapter 5: Flying Above Life's Financial Hurdles 95

Chapter 6: Healing Life's Damaged Wings 113

Chapter 7: Fertilizing Life's Spiritual Garden 125

Chapter 8: Avoiding Spiritual Plane Crashes 139

Chapter 9: The Power of Your Mind to Renew Itself 153

Chapter 10: The Power to 'Peck' Into Destiny 173

Chapter 11: Changing From a Sunset Mentality

to a Sunrise Mentality 185

Chapter 12: The Power to accept and Receive

Life's Inheritance 199

Chapter 13: Plugging Into Life's Energy Outlet 215

Conclusion: Completing the Journey 227

Introduction

As you read *The Solution Oriented Mind*, allow your thoughts to explore the endless possibilities of the human mind. You will realize that only people with the right concepts of life will be able to experience their blessings to the fullest in spite of physical and mental obstacles. What life requires of us – in order for us to fully have access to every possible solution – is a clear vision of the power of our mind. It is capable of finding a meaningful solution to every major challenge we face on a daily basis. It is capable of finding a miraculous solution for every single problem in the universe. Once you discover the power of your mind, you will fully understand that there are no challenges that cannot be overcome. Unless we understand the dynamics of this great mind that God has placed in us, it's going to be hard to put our faith in action and strongly believe that there is no mountain in life that can't be conquered.

Solutions are readily accessible to all solution oriented minds desiring to boldly put their faith in action. By having a solution oriented mind, you will be able to experience the manifestations of life in a much broader spectrum. As a result, not only you will see miracles take place in your life, you will also become a walking miracle through the venues of the Holy

Spirit. You will be able to function like a sharp and powerful human instrument demonstrating the power and favors of God's miraculous kingdom on Earth.

The reason why solution oriented people are able to experience the power of God is because they always have the desire to fly high. They don't allow their problems to define who they are. Somehow, they know they can fly; they know that the higher they fly spiritually, the more they will be able to explore and enjoy the beauty of the sky.

By making you conscious of the magnitude of the solution oriented mind, I really want to instill in you the desire to fly higher in the realm of the spirit. The higher we fly spiritually, the more we see the manifestation of God's glory. I want to encourage you to think about the endless possibilities before you as you allow your mind to become solution oriented.

In Matthew 6:33, Jesus said; "Seek ye first the kingdom of God, and His righteousness; and all these things shall be added unto you." That's His way of inspiring you to allow the power of His kingdom to overshadow you so you can use your spiritual energy efficiently. As we do likewise, our needs will inevitably be met. Again, I want to draw your attention to the power that is readily available to you when you become solution oriented.

God created our minds with the power to find even miraculous solutions when we focus our attention not on our problems but on the solutions to our problems. This is something we have to constantly train our minds to do in order for our thoughts to be channeled properly

In the *Solution Oriented Mind*, I encourage you to enjoy the sky where you fly in order to explore the power of God in a more meaningful and productive way. You will discover that your mind has the power to make the impossible become more than possible. Your success will be proportionate with your willingness to allow your mind to become solution oriented.

In this book, I encourage you to turn your pains into praise through a positive change of mentality and focus. As you maintain an attitude of praise in your daily routine, you will be able to fly high in every important area of your life. Having a solution oriented mind will help you maintain an attitude of praise in everything that you do; and success will follow.

Chapter 1:

Flying above Life's Challenges

Your challenges constitute the toughest hurdles of your life. Every human being on Earth is subject to some challenges. They are almost inevitable. This chapter will equip you spiritually in order to develop the coping skills to make the most out of those difficult moments. Experience reveals that challenges and midnight situations, when you approach them with the right frame of mind, may yield your greatest blessings in life.

As you prepare your heart and mind to renew your strength for a higher dimension of faith in your spiritual walk, be ready for God to accomplish five things in your life that will pave the way for a miraculous journey with Him. (a) He will increase your sustaining power. (b) He will renew your strength. (c) He will make you "soar on wings like eagles." (d) He will make you "run and not grow weary." (e) He will make you "walk and not grow faint."

The prophet Isaiah presents a clear picture of how God paves the way for us to fly above our darkest hours. He uses the eagle's analogy because, in order to fly above our midnight situations, we need the strength, the power, and the wings of an eagle. Notice what Isaiah said:

Do you not know? Have you not heard?
The LORD is the everlasting God,

the Creator of the ends of the Earth.

He will not grow tired or weary,

and his understanding no one can fathom.

He gives strength to the weary and increases the power of the

weak. Even youth grow tired and weary,

and young men stumble and fall;

But, those who hope in the LORD will renew their strength. They will soar on wings like eagles; they will run and not grow weary, they will walk and not be faint. Isaiah 40:28-31

As you reflect on the following meaningful lessons we may learn from eagles, see how you may apply them to your personal quest to experience those five promises. This will ensure that, instead of being discouraged and depressed over what you can't do, you'll make a commitment to refocus your attention on what you are able to do through Christ, who strengthens you. Instead of being imprisoned by your problems, you will be able to fly above them spiritually. God will grant you the serenity to go through life with a different frame of mind. You will experience peace even in the midst of your darkest hours. In this chapter, you will be asked to be eagle-minded in order to experience a new mentality that will open your eyes to the endless possibilities God has placed before you.

Eagle-minded people are those who have developed the coping skills to remain peaceful while experiencing the darkest moments of their existence. Instead of focusing their attention on their pains, they focus it on the everlasting and sublime possibilities of the kingdom of God. In other words, they are kingdom-minded believers. They are willing and ready to "soar on wings like eagles." They raise their faith above logic, knowing that by faith even our biggest obstacles can be removed. Through communion with God you will acquire a higher dimension of spirituality that will give you power over any major roadblocks in your life. Through communion with God, you will develop these qualities:

- **Eagles fly at high altitude** - Your faith will allow you to fly high in your spiritual journey. The greater your faith, the more you will see great things accomplished in your life. The higher you fly spiritually, the more you will explore the blessings of God's kingdom. You will, in due season, be empowered to experience growth in every significant area of your life. In reality, eagles were not supposed to fly so high; their weight was supposed to intimidate them from flying high. But, eagles are naturally very strategic, focused, and goal oriented. They believe that they can fly high in spite of major difficulties. That's the "one-hundred-degree attitude."

Tim Dumler's experience

A motivational products company interviewed Tim Dumler by phone for a sales job. He informed them that his goal was to become their number one employee. However, after meeting him in person they were shocked to discover he was legally blind. But he promised he'd buy a machine that magnifies letters. So, despite serious misgivings, they hired him. And it's a good thing they did. He came in early, worked late, and within six years became their top producer. His clients loved him because when you're blind you become a great listener. And his associates loved him because of his caring, positive attitude. He said, "It's unfortunate that I'm visually impaired but adversity made me a better person. I have a lot more than I don't have." Tim has the one-hundred-degree attitude! What's the one-hundred-degree attitude? Motivational speaker Mack Anderson explains: At ninety-nine degrees Celsius, water is hot. At one-hundred degrees, it boils. With boiling water comes steam. And steam can power a train. One extra degree makes all the difference in business and in life; it separates the good from the great.

- **Eagles have strong vision.** No wonder it is often said that eagles can see a mouse from miles above the Earth. They have the ability to focus on something up to three miles away. They remain focused until they reach their prey. This teaches us that we must remain focused in our prayers, and strongly believe that God will allow us to reach our goals. We may encounter some hard times, but if we remain focused, God will honor our perseverance.

Obstacles should serve as stepping stones on our road to victory. When you really have a vision, no matter how impossible it appears to others, you still have the motivation to maintain your fight until your last breath, because the factors that motivate you should never be around you, but in you. If you encounter anyone who says, "I had a vision, but somehow, I've lost my motivation," it simply means they did not really have a vision. If you really have a vision, it will build in you the urge to fight until your last breath. As you read the following story, try to see what it will take for you to bring your vision, or your dream to pass.

> "I had a vision, but somehow, I've lost my motivation," it simply means they did not have a vision.

A swimmer once asked his coach, "When will I get my Olympic gold medal?" The coach took him to the pool, held his head under water until he began to struggle. Then he said, "This is your answer." He went on to tell him that he'd get his gold medal when he wanted to be the best in his sport as desperately as he wanted to get his breath of air.

This story briefly illustrates, not only the necessity to have a goal, a dream, or a vision, but the passion, perseverance and commitment required to make it reality.

- **Eagles feed on fresh prey.** Notice what Jesus said: "Man shall not live by bread alone, but by every word that proceeds out of the mouth of God." You should feed daily on the fresh manna of the word of God. Occupy your thoughts and conversations with His promises. You will be amazed to see how they will come to pass in your life. Whatever we allow to occupy our mind, thoughts and words on a regular basis, controls to a great extent what we accomplish. Like eagles, you should feed daily on the fresh prey of the word of God. It will build the confidence and personal conviction you need in order to fulfill your purpose. Immediately after reading the following paragraph, I was convinced that this is what it takes to fully inherit the blessings of God's kingdom. You have to develop an "A" mentality, while refusing to settle for less:

Students who refused to settle for less

You probably heard the meaningful story of a professor who stood before his class of thirty senior molecular biology students while holding the final exam in his hand. Right before he passed it out he told his students, "I have been privileged to be your instructor this semester, and I know how hard you have worked to prepare for this test. I also know most of you are off to medical school or graduate school next autumn. I am well aware of how much pressure you are under to keep your grade point averages up. Because I am confident that you know this material, I am prepared to offer an automatic B to anyone who opts to skip taking the final exam." The relief was audible. A number of students jumped up from their desks, thanking the professor for the lifeline he had thrown them. "Any other takers?" he asked. "This is your last opportunity." One more student decided to go. The instructor then handed out the final exam, which consisted of two sentences. It read: "Congratulations, you have just received an A in this class. Keep believing in yourself."

It was a just reward for the students who had worked hard and believed in themselves. What a difference it makes to cherish an "A" mentality. It gives you the automatic urge to aim at excellence in everything you do. Thus, I admonish you, like eagles, to feed only on fresh prey of the word of God daily in order to maintain your confidence and the courage to strive for excellence in everything you do.

- **Eagles enjoy turbulent weather.** Eagles throw a party when they see a storm coming. They celebrate the storm. They know it's going to cause them to rise higher. They use the force of the wind to fly higher above the clouds. This allows them to rest their wings as they glide above the storm. While other birds look for places to hide from the storm, eagles see it as an excellent opportunity to rise higher.

As an eagle-minded believer, you can use the storms of your life to rise to greater heights. The reason why God allows you to experience storms in your life is to strengthen you and prepare you for greater accomplishments. If you pass the test, you will later thank God even for the storms. You will realize that were it not for the storm, you would not be so blessed. Think about Joseph who told his brothers that God blessed him so abundantly because of what they did to him. He even told them not to apologize to him, because their betrayal was the principal bridge to his rise to power over Egypt. This should serve as a great and meaningful lesson for us in our hardships.

Henry Ford made a meaningful statement worth heeding. "Problems only exist for solutions," he said. That's why many great men and women achieve their greatest accomplishments during the toughest times in their lives. Cervantes wrote *Don*

Quixote while in jail. John Bunyan wrote *Pilgrim's Progress* while in jail. When Thomas Edison invented the phonograph, he was almost completely deaf. It used to amuse him that other people had to shout to talk to him, saying, "A man who has to shout can never tell a lie."

God, through His Word, nature and experience, teaches us that His blessings are for those who are willing to go the extra mile. There is a story about an early 20th-century London newspaper ad by famous South Pole explorer Sir Ernest Shackleton, which stated the following: "Men wanted for hazardous journey. Small wages, bitter cold, long months of complete darkness, constant danger. Safe return is doubtful." The response was so overwhelming that Shackleton wrote later, "It seemed as though all the men in Great Britain were determined to accompany us." How many have the courage, and are just waiting for the opportunity and a leader with a vision to go the extra mile?

We must never allow our negative feelings to blind our eyes from the opportunities that are placed before us. We are told that there was a distinguished singer who was scheduled to perform at the Grand Opera House. The concert hall was packed. Suddenly the house manager announced, "Ladies and gentlemen, I regret that due to illness our special guest will be unable to perform this evening. But we've found another singer, an equally great talent, so would you please give her a warm welcome." The crowd groaned so loudly that nobody even heard the singer's name. You could feel the disappointment everywhere. The stand-in singer gave it everything she had. But when she finished only one child stood up in the balcony and shouted, "Mommy, I think you're wonderful!" Realizing what took place, the crowd jumped to their feet and gave her a standing ovation that lasted for several minutes.

This teaches us that, like eagles, we must understand that there is an opportunity to rise higher even in the midst of turbulent storms.

- **Eagles test before they trust.** Dr. Myles Munroe, in his seven principles of eagles, relates the following: "When a female eagle meets a male and they want to mate, she flies down to Earth with the male pursuing her and she picks a twig. She flies back into the air with the male pursuing her. Once she has reached a height high enough for her, she lets the twig fall to the ground and watches it as it falls. The male chases after the twig. The faster it falls, the faster he chases it. He has to catch it before it falls to the ground. He then brings it back to the female eagle. The female eagle grabs the twig and flies to a higher altitude and then drops the twig for the male to chase. This goes on for hours, with the height increasing until the female eagle is assured that the male eagle has mastered the art of catching the twig which shows commitment. Then and only then, will she allow him to mate with her."

I think we should apply this principle to all human relationships whether it be in marriage, business or work. We need to test people in all walks of life before making any serious commitment. However, as far as God is concerned, we can trust Him one hundred percent. His love and commitment have been tested and demonstrated in every way possible through His son, Jesus-Christ. He even gave His life on the cross for you. He did what no human being would be willing to do for you. That's why He deserves your trust. You can trust Him to do for you what you can't do for yourself.

> You can trust Him to do for you what you can't do for yourself.

- **When an Eagle grows old, his feathers become weak and cannot take him as fast as he should go.** When he feels weak and is about to die, he retires to a place far away in the rocks. While there, he plucks out every feather on his body until he is completely bare. He stays in this hiding place until he has grown new feathers, then he can come out. This shows the need for spiritual renewal, which we all need in due season in order to maintain a balanced life. On day two the focus will be mainly on what to do in order to experience spiritual renewal that God promised us in Isaiah 40: 28–31.

Reflect on the areas of your life where you need renewal, and while asking God to help you in the process, make a commitment for improvement on a regular basis. In your spiritual voyage, you need to do this often. You need to pray for God to provide you the strength to renew your relationship with Him on a higher dimension, which will equip you to remove the mountains of your life. By renewing your spirituality, you will acquire enough wisdom and experience to gradually practice the principles of success within the kingdom of God. By allowing yourself time to experience renewal, you will regain your strength in every area of your life; your faith will expand, allowing you the possibility of personal growth as well as realizing your vision.

> He already knows you have what it takes to succeed.

Spiritual renewal also paves the way for a better relationship with the Lord. That's why He told His people: _I carried you on eagles' wings and brought you to myself._ Exodus 19:4. Only spiritual renewal can make such a powerful connection with God accessible. It opens the door for God to bring us to Him as He carries us on eagles' wings.

Spiritual renewal allows you to discover who you really are, as well as the natural qualities God created within you. He already knows what those qualities are. He already knows you have what it takes to succeed. There is nothing that He is going to learn about you, because He already knows exactly who you are. He just wants you to know who you are and what your purpose is so that he may empower you to use your potential wisely and efficiently.

DESIRING SPIRITUAL RENEWAL – In order to experience spiritual renewal, you must first desire it. Your life will dictate to you from time to time when you really need it. You need it mostly when you're seeking God's guidance in a particular situation where the road is blurry before your eyes. In those moments, God's miraculous intervention is your best way out.

PRAYING FOR SPIRITUAL RENEWAL – Praying for spiritual renewal should never be spontaneous. It must be systematic. It is a process for which you should create precious time in your daily activities. I suggest that you take at least an hour early in the morning before you engage in any activity for that purpose. That's what will equip you to acquire the peace and wisdom you need to follow the road ahead.

FASTING FOR SPIRITUAL RENEWAL – Fasting is extremely important for anyone seeking deeper spiritual renewal. It allows you to create time, not only for prayer, but for partial or total abstinence from foods, activities, or anything that may hinder your spirituality. The power of a spiritual fast is so remarkable that it should be a priority in your schedule as you go through life. Its benefits are beyond explanation.

> Most of our limits don't come from God, but within us.

As you pray today for God to help you enlarge your vision toward flying above your midnight situations, pray also for Him to help you unleash your potential effectively in everything you do. You will inevitably reap the benefits. The following helps us understand what can take place when you discover and unleash your potential.

There was a time when Spain possessed the territory on both sides of the Straits of Gibraltar. So, on their coins they stamped the two Pillars of Hercules, which is what the two promontories of rock were called.

Then came the discovery of the New World, and with it the

realization that there was in fact something else out there. So they changed the coins to read, "More beyond." Seeing yourself as a flying eagle through faith in Christ will help to enlarge your vision like Spain did. Most of our limits don't come from God, but within us. As you look at your life, has fear or some other negative thing burned into it? Or, are you convinced that there is indeed more beyond, and that you're going to reach out for it? Your answer to this question may determine your level of faith in God as you prepare to be a flying eagle.

Today I'd like for us to reflect on five things that make eagles fly higher than other birds. Those same principles from eagles may be applied in your life for various reasons. After reading them, try to answer the following questions.

1. Why is it necessary for God's children to know their natural abilities?

_____

_____

_____

_____

_____

2. Why is it necessary to use our energy wisely even in our missionary endeavors?

_____

_____

_____

_____

_____

3. What do eagles teach us about taking it one day at a time?

_____

_____

_____

_____

_____

4. What are the primary definitions of the word PATIENCE?

_____

_____

_____

_____

_____

5. Explain when and why we need to stop sometimes in order to fast for spiritual energy and sustaining power?

_____

_____

_____

_____

Five things that make eagles fly higher than other birds

1. **Eagles are created to fly high.** They always have the willingness and motivation to fly high. In order for God to change your situation, you must change your perspective and believe that He created you to fly high. Without this strong conviction that you can make it if you try, it will be impossible for you to accomplish anything great in your life. Most of the boundaries that hinder our progress are self-built. Once you nourish within your heart the belief that, by God's grace, you can fly, you will begin to witness the miraculous unfolding of your endless possibilities. You will begin to realize He created you with what you need to succeed.

2. **Eagles conserve energy by gliding in thermal wind currents.** They can achieve speeds of up to 50 mph. If you use your talents and energy wisely, you will be able to accomplish more with less effort. Sometimes people complain about doing so much while accomplishing so little. This, in itself, is enough to discourage anyone seeking to make progress in any field in life. Whenever that happens, you know they have not been using their talents and energy wisely. If this ever happens to you, the first thing you need to do is to pray for wisdom like King Solomon. Secondly, reconsider your strategies, and practice doing things systematically instead of emotionally and randomly. Like eagles, you will accomplish more with less effort. It's okay to put a lot of energy and effort in everything we do, but we have to do it wisely.

3. **Eagles travel up to 180 miles a day.** Patience will give you the courage to go through life expecting God to bestow His blessings on you in due season. Without it you will experience discouragement and burnouts to the level of letting go of your goals and motivation. You must practice doing one thing at a time, leaving the timing of the results in God's hands. You will reap the blessings in due season.

I like the following definitions of the word patience from Random House Webster's College Dictionary:

- The bearing of provocation, annoyance, misfortune, or pain without complaint, loss of temper, or anger.
- An ability or willingness to suppress restlessness or annoyance when confronted with delay.
- Quiet, steady perseverance; even-tempered care; diligence.

These definitions tell us that 'patience' is not just a simple word; it is a principle that we must live by. We can travel a limitless number of miles if we practice perseverance, allowing the process to pave the way for miraculous results at the appropriate timing.

4. **Eagles can fly as high as 10,000 feet.** Because the God you serve is the Master of the universe, by believing in Him, and trusting Him, you can accomplish great things in your journey. So, believe, claim, and accept your victory by faith. Notice what Jesus said to the skeptical Martha, Lazarus' sister: "Did I not tell you that if you believe, you will see the glory of God?"– *John 11:40*.

The power of God can only be demonstrated through faith in those who truly believe that God created them to have a successful life. It's amazing how just a change of attitude can give us a fresh orientation, allowing us to see things in a different frame of mind. All of a sudden you realize that you have tremendous potential you thought you never had. You begin to accomplish things you would never imagine you are capable of doing. This only takes place after you allow God to change your mentality. It allows you to focus more on the positive side of life than the negative. Your thought pattern focuses more upward than downward. That's how you experience the manifestation of God's power.

5. **Eagles migrate when their fishing waters freeze over.** There are times when we may become complacent in our spiritual journey. We may realize that our relationship with God 'freezes.' It's time to start fasting for power and spiritual energy in order to continue to fly to greater spiritual heights. Find a quiet place to spend more time with your creator in order to recharge your spiritual battery. You can do this in the tranquility of your room alone, or any place where it's easy for you to pray and meditate without any interruption. I like to go to a public park early in the morning. Public parks usually have secluded areas where you can read, meditate, and pray. If you can find time to do this, the benefits will be great. Nature provides a sea of inspiration and motivation that cannot be undermined. I encourage you to do that whenever you sense

that your spiritual fishing waters have frozen over.

Having learned so many practical lessons from eagles, I think we should apply them in our daily walk with God. They have the ingredients to help acquire the right mentality in order for our prayers to remove mountains of difficulties in our life. As eagle-minded and kingdom-minded believers whose petitions are kingdom-focused, you will serve God on a higher dimension. All your prayer requests should focus on receiving and enjoying the blessings of the kingdom of God. They should focus on flying higher in your spiritual journey. In other words, you have to aim at flying high. You have to digest this concept so deeply that it becomes a part of who you are.

> In order to fly high, you have to be willing to do so.

In order to fly high, you have to be willing to do so. You should accept the fact that God has already equipped you to fly high. You can fly high, and you will fly high. Like the eagle, God created you to fly high.

Points worth special attention

- By occupying your thoughts with the blessings of life daily instead of its problems, you will become a solution minded person.

- Solution oriented people move mountains, because their faith opens their eyes to life's fortune instead of misfortune.
- When you focus on the solutions to your problems, you will face them with the assurance that they will be solved, no matter how impossible they are.

Notes

_____
_____
_____
_____
_____
_____
_____
_____
_____
_____
_____
_____
_____

Chapter 2:

Turning Life's Setbacks into a Ladder to Success

I call this spiritual concept, "The Spider's Approach." It centers primarily on the web-building techniques of spiders. Later in this chapter you will discover how spiders use their setbacks to build better webs with magnificent designs. This approach is similar to Abraham Lincoln's in terms of adaptation to life's challenges. As one of the most successful and influential presidents in U.S. history, Abraham Lincoln has truly been a great inspiration to anyone seeking to pursue a meaningful venture. Thousands of books have been written about his tenacity and perseverance in spite of his setbacks. His roadmap to the presidency, perhaps, was the hardest and longest, but it did not stop him from pursuing his dream. His diligence and persistence have always been a center of focus for scholars worldwide. He led this nation successfully during a tumultuous period of its history – the Civil War. His setbacks never discouraged him on his quest for the presidency of the United States of America. Instead, he used them as an inspirational ladder that he climbed in order to achieve his goal. As we consider the spider's approach to life challenges, we may compare it with that of Abraham Lincoln.

Like Lincoln, spiders are not afraid of setbacks and hard work. Their webs can be about 20 times bigger than the spiders themselves. They have the tenacity to fight until their goal is reached. They have the patience to start over and over again if they have to. The following is a vivid description of a spider's tenacity and persistence:

After the radials are complete, the spider fortifies the center of the web with about five circular threads. Then a spiral of non-sticky, widely spaced threads is made to enable the spider to move easily around its own web during construction, working from the inside out. Then, beginning from the outside in, the spider methodically replaces this spiral with another, more closely spaced one of adhesive threads. It uses the initial radiating lines as well as the non-sticky spirals as guide lines. The spaces between each spiral and the next are directly proportional to the distance from the tip of its back legs to its spinners. This is one way the spider uses its own body as a measuring/spacing device. While the sticky spirals are formed, the non-adhesive spirals are removed as there is no need for them anymore.

Spiders illustrate very well the life and tenacity of Lincoln before becoming president in 1860. He experienced an unprecedented number of setbacks in his life that set him apart from other presidents in various ways. Here's the road he traveled before becoming president:

Lincoln had two business ventures that failed, lost eight

elections, and had a complete nervous breakdown before becoming president in 1860. His story is inspirational and shows that if you keep moving toward your dream, you will eventually make it. Lincoln overcame great setbacks and obstacles on his journey. Take a look at the synopsis of his life and see whether you would have had the courage to continue on.

1809 - Born on February 12, 1809.

1816 - His family was forced out of their home and he needed to work to support them.

1818 - His mother passed away.

1828 - His sister died.

1831 - A business venture failed.

1832 - He ran for the State Legislature and lost.

1832 - In the same year, he also lost his job. He decided he wanted to go to law school but couldn't get in.

1833 - He borrowed money from a friend to start a business. By the end of the year, he was bankrupt.

1834 - He ran for the State Legislature again, and this time he won.

1835 - The year was looking better as he was engaged to be married. Unfortunately, his fiancée died and he was grief-stricken.

1836 - This was the year he had a nervous breakdown and for six months was bedridden.

1836 - He sought to become Speaker of the State Legislature. He was defeated.

1840 - He sought to become Elector. He was defeated.

1842- He married Mary Todd. They had four boys but only one would live to maturity.

1843 - He ran for Congress and lost, but was finally elected in 1846.

1848 - He ran for re-election to Congress. He lost.

1849 - He sought the job of Land Officer in his home state. He didn't get the job.

1850 - His son, Edward, died.

1854 - He ran for U.S. Senate and lost.

1856 - He sought the vice presidential nomination at a national convention. He got less than 100 votes.

1858 - He ran for the Senate again, and lost.

1860 - Lincoln is elected President of the United States.

What a journey! This is indeed what the spider's approach is all about: Refusing to take NO for an answer. The word of God gives us numerous reasons why we should never take NO for an answer. As you meditate on them, allow the Holy Spirit to strengthen and enhance your faith so that you may pursue your dream in spite of obstacles, setbacks, and stumbling blocks. Like Abraham Lincoln, the human spider, we should build our web on God's promises with the assurance that He will richly reward our perseverance.

The spider's approach calls for steadfastness and boldness that cause us to stand firm and unmovable in spite of numerous obstacles. Notice what Paul said: *Stand firm. Let nothing move you. Always give yourselves fully to the work of the Lord, because you know that your labor in the Lord is not in vain. I pray that out of his glorious riches he may strengthen you with power through his Spirit in your inner being, so that Christ may dwell in your hearts through faith. And I pray that you, being rooted and established in love, may have power, together with all the Lord's holy people, to grasp how wide and long and high and deep is the love of Christ, and to know this love that surpasses knowledge—that you may be filled to the measure of all the fullness of God.* Ephesians 3:16–19. Being rooted and grounded in God's Holy Word will pave the way for his power to be active in your

> God's Holy word will pave the way for his power to be active in your life

life. This generates a boldness of action in you that keeps you motivated no matter how much resistance you encounter. What happens at this stage is that your trust in God and the wonder-working power of His Holy Spirit have reached a climax that does not bow down to any resistance. This is part of the lessons we learn from spiders.

1. **Spiders build their webs with steadfastness and purpose.** They know that insects will get trapped in their webs, providing nutrition to them. The challenges you face today may be your meals tomorrow. The reason why millions start a good project and never finish it could be because of a lack of steadfastness and boldness of action. They lose interest or tend to get discouraged as they encounter major setbacks. Steadfastness is the mental energy that keeps you going without ever wanting to quit. That's why Paul said: Stand firm; let nothing move you. If you allow it, an obstacle can have the power to discourage you or even stop you, because you've lost your enthusiasm. So, like spiders, be steadfast and unmovable as you seek to reach your goal or fulfill your dream.

2. **Spiders are hard and efficient workers.** I am sure you're familiar with the adage, no pain, no gain. As simple as it

sounds, it is a principle we must live by. It simply means that hard work pays off, People who refuse to work hard will not accomplish much in spite of talents, skills, training, and education.

Hard work helps you develop the character and strength you need to persevere in your tasks. Notice how spiders diligently fabricate silk in order to keep their bodies and eggs safe. They know if they become lazy and stop the process there will be a lot at stake. They continue with it laboriously until their web is completed. I have no way of knowing what tasks you have ahead of you; but I do know if you are determined to work as hard as a spider, by God's grace, you will be able to complete it.

3. **Spiders are excellent manufacturers who know their natural abilities.** They are capable of producing their own silk from their spinneret glands located at the tip of their abdomen. Each gland manufactures a thread for a specific purpose – they produce a sticky silk for trapping prey and a fine silk for wrapping the prey. They are capable of manufacturing various types of silk for different purposes. Human beings should learn this lesson from spiders before we embark on any projects, career, or even ministry. We should

find out what our God-given talents or natural abilities are. We should find out what line of work corresponds better with our natural abilities. In this sense, our energy will not be wasted, and we will enjoy what we do. Millions of people go to work from day to day with a feeling of unhappiness, simply because they don't like what they do. The pay check is the only thing they appreciate about their work. However, if they only took time to discover and unfold their natural abilities they would reap huge benefits.

Remember that understanding your natural abilities:
- Helps you to enjoy what you do.
- Gives you a stamina that's almost automatic as you work.
- Causes you to be more productive with less effort.
- Creates your bridge to success in spite of your shortcomings.

The following story of Charles Zibelman's dream illustrates this point very well. Charles Zibelman's dream was to be famous as a long-distance swimmer. He trained intensively and began making sports headlines with his amazing aquatic achievements. First, he established an endurance record by swimming for eighty hours consecutively. Then, near Honolulu, he swam for one hundred continuous hours. Still not content, he decided to attempt to swim the Hudson River from Albany to New York

City. Battling hunger, fatigue and sleepiness, he amazed everyone by completing the one-hundred forty-seven mile trip nonstop. Zibelman is still regarded as the most outstanding long-distance swimmer because he not only taught himself to swim, but had no legs!

Knowing your natural abilities is so important that I strongly believe everyone needs to place a major emphasis on it. One of the best ways to discover your natural God-given abilities, is to carefully evaluate your activities in order to depict what you enjoy doing well with less effort. You will notice that you are inspired and naturally equipped as you conduct those activities. You don't feel the urge to just hurry up and get them out of the way. You want to do them almost as perfectly as possible. You become more and more productive. You're not so concerned about approval; you just want to perform well. That's a strong indication you are functioning within the framework of your natural abilities.

4. **Spiders use their energy wisely.** They use their webs so efficiently and skillfully that they can catch their prey effortlessly. They use their energy to build the web, knowing that a well-constructed web will allow them to trap their food without using too much energy.

Your level of blessings is determined by how well you manufacture your spiritual web. The more effort you put into it by using your energy wisely, the more efficient it will be in terms of bringing and holding life's blessings to you. By this I mean every good thing you desire for yourself or your family would come your way irrefutably. Take time to pray as you plan your future, because God will not provide any blessing to you that you're not ready to receive.

As you decide to work harder, make sure you use your energy wisely. It hurts to find out that you haven't accomplished much after putting so much energy and effort into what you do. Some people become powerless and lose focus after realizing their hard works amount to almost nothing.

5. **Spiders are task oriented.** They work diligently at constructing their webs while staying focused throughout the process. This is done by letting out a first fine adhesive thread to drift on the faintest breeze across a gap. When it sticks to a surface at the far end, this is felt by a change in the vibrations transmitted back to the spider; the spider then reels in and tighten the first strand, then carefully walks along it and strengthens it with a second thread. This process is repeated until the thread is strong enough to support the rest of the web.

Whatever your calling may be in life, if you focus on the accomplishment of your tasks with devotion and commitment, God will reward your effort beyond your expectation. As you read through the Bible, you can easily see how God rewards faithful servants who show great devotion and commitment in what they do. God counts them as faithful stewards.

Bible Reading Exercise

As you meditate on the parable of the bags of gold that was told by Jesus Christ, pay special attention to how God rewards devotion and commitment in our daily tasks as His stewards on Earth.

Again, it will be like a man going on a journey, who called his servants and entrusted his wealth to them. To one he gave five bags of gold, to another two bags, and to another one bag, each according to his ability. Then he went on his journey. The man who had received five bags of gold went at once and put his money to work and gained five bags more. So also, the one with two bags of gold gained two more. But the man who had received one bag went off, dug a hole in the ground and hid his master's money. After a long time the master of those servants returned and settled accounts with them. The man who had received five bags of gold brought the other five. 'Master,' he said, 'you entrusted me with five bags of gold. See, I have gained five more. His master replied, 'Well done, good and faithful servant! You have been faithful with a few things; I will put you in charge of many things. Come and share your master's happiness!'

The man with two bags of gold also came. 'Master,' he said, 'you entrusted me with two bags of gold; see, I have gained two more.'

His master replied, 'Well done, good and faithful servant! You have been faithful with a few things; I will put you in charge of many things. Come and share your master's happiness!'

Then the man who had received one bag of gold came. 'Master,' he said, 'I knew that you are a hard man, harvesting where you have not sown and gathering where you have not scattered seed. So I was afraid and went out and hid your gold in the ground. See, here is what belongs to you.'

His master replied, 'You wicked, lazy servant! So you knew that I harvest where I have not sown and gather where I have not scattered seed? Well then, you should have put my money on deposit with the bankers, so that when I returned I would have received it back with interest."

"'So take the bag of gold from him and give it to the one who has ten bags. For whoever has will be given more, and they will have an abundance. Whoever does not have, even what they have will be *taken from them. And throw that worthless servant outside, into the darkness, where there will be weeping and gnashing of teeth.'* - Matthew 25:14–30

The spider's approach is what gave those faithful servants the courage and steadfastness to work diligently. They received great rewards from their master for doing so. Whatever your talents are, God can use them mightily to His honor and glory if you are willing to be used by Him. The wicked and lazy servant thought his master was unfair by not given him enough talent. What he failed to realized was that, it's not how much you have that matters, but what you do with what you have. You might think that your talents are not meaningful enough for you to make a great impact. However, you need to know that sometimes good things come in small packages. Don't worry about the size of your package; leave it faithfully in God's hands and allow Him to use you as you put your faith to work. Work diligently at putting your talents to work, and He certainly will do the rest.

> Sometimes good things come in small packages

Points worth special attention

- Erase the word failure from your vocabulary. There is no such thing as failure for those who try. What appears to be a failure is just one more step toward your victory.

- When you feel like you're about to be discouraged, use the spider's approach by allowing your setbacks to create better designs for your web.
- Don't worry too much about results; just enjoy your journey as you work diligently toward your goal. Those who focus too much on results tend to get discouraged along the way.
- Find out what your God-given abilities are and build your career on them. You will enjoy what you do, and in turn, you will accomplish more with less effort.
- Don't worry about the size of your talents. What matters to God is what you do with what He has entrusted to you.

Notes

_____
_____
_____
_____
_____
_____
_____

Chapter 3:

Getting Rid of Fear

When we consider the source of fear, we may easily trace it to a lack of faith in God and His infinite power. When we don't have faith in God, it's easy for fear to paralyze us physically, mentally, and spiritually. The opposite is also true: When we have faith in God, fear cannot influence us because we know He has power even over the storms of our lives. In fact, storms are a major platform for Him to manifest His power and glory.

Jesus spent His entire earthly ministry trying to get rid of fear in the life of His disciples knowing that it could paralyze their faith and action. That's the principal reason why He asked them: *Why are ye so fearful, O ye of little faith?* Today, I invite you to begin asking the Lord to help you eliminate all traces of fear in your life in order for you to experience the wonder working power of His Holy Spirit.

For years, experts have been wondering why chickens can't really fly. The answer may be summarized in one single word: fear. Chickens can't fly because they have developed the fear of flying. Many believers do not experience God's power because they have developed the fear of trying.

Veterinary experts give us the primary reasons why chickens can't fly:

- Chickens are adapted to living on the ground. It is customary for them to conduct all their activities on the ground.

- Chickens' beaks are better adapted to pecking off the ground. Their beaks point to the ground, making it easier for them to peck off the ground.
- Chickens' feet are better adapted to walking instead of perching. They have not developed the habit of lifting them off the ground to fly.
- Chickens' wings have not been developed. Lack of practice causes their wings not to develop the strength and ability to fly.
- Chickens' wings are smaller than other birds their size. In spite of being big birds, their wings remain relatively small.
- Chickens have developed the fear of flying.

We may summarize all of the reasons above into one single word: fear. Because chickens are adapted to living on the ground, they develop the fear of flying. Fear keeps them from enjoying the flying experience. That's what happens to us when we become so adapted to our present situations. We become so pessimistic that we fail to try anything new with a different perspective on life. As you read this today, make up your mind to recharge your spiritual battery and build up your faith in order to experience the blessings of God. They have been made available to you; but your attachment to the ground may cause you not to have access to them. Just as chickens' beaks are accustomed to pecking off the ground, there are some habits that we grew up with that may hinder our progress, because they make us look down instead of up. As followers of Jesus Christ we have a great advantage: We have been called to look up to our savior for all the provisions that are needed for doing the will of God. We should make sure that our beaks point up regularly.

You've read that chickens don't fly because their wings are smaller than other birds of their size. Think about us as believers – our spiritual wings are proportional to our level of faith. The greater our faith, the bigger our wings will be. The point I'm trying to make is that serving God is not enough; you must exercise your faith in order to develop your spiritual wings and fly higher. Some Christians have chickens' wings, others have eagle's wings. Christians with chickens' wings will never be able to fly higher than chickens. However, Christians with eagles' wings will be able to fly and soar on wings like eagles. They are the ones who greatly benefit from the blessings of God's kingdom. My question to you is: How high do you want to fly?

> The greater our faith, the bigger our wings will be

In the space provided below, list all the things you want to accomplish in your life. Revisit it several times to make sure that's what you want to accomplish, and then in your daily devotion always present that list to God asking Him to provide you with the faith and strength to bring it to pass. Never let a day go by without fulfilling a portion of that list. Fear will attempt to make you doubt sometimes; just ignore that feeling and keep moving.

Bible Reading Exercise One

Read and meditate on the following Bible stories. In the first story, you will see that even the biggest storms in your life can be a platform for your miracles if you choose to maintain your trust in God. This should help you realize that everything in the universe is under His control. You will also understand that everything happens for a reason.

Then he got into the boat and his disciples followed him. Suddenly, a furious storm came up on the lake, so that the waves swept over the boat. But Jesus was sleeping. The disciples went and woke him, saying, "Lord, save us! We're going to drown!"

He replied, "You of little faith, why are you so afraid?" Then he got up and rebuked the winds and the waves, and it was completely calm.

The men were amazed and asked, "What kind of man is this?

Even the winds and the waves obey him!" – Matthew 25:23-27.

Questions for Exercise One

1. What did the disciples do when the waves swept over the boat?

___

___

___

___

2. What was the Lord's answer to the disciples' request?

___

___

___

___

3. In your own words, explain why Jesus told them: "O ye of little faith." Write down the things in your life that cause you to experience fear sometimes. Next, write down how you plan to cope with fear based on what you've learned thus far.

___

___

___

4. What would the disciples have done if they really had faith in God?

_____

_____

_____

_____

Bible Reading Exercise Two - Numbers 13:17–33

When Moses sent them to explore Canaan, he said, "Go up through the Negev and on into the hill country. See what the land is like and whether the people who live there are strong or weak, few or many. 19 What kind of land do they live in? Is it good or bad? What kind of towns do they live in? Are they unwalled or fortified? 20 How is the soil? Is it fertile or poor? Are there trees in it or not? Do your best to bring back some of the fruit of the land." (It was the season for the first ripe grapes.)

So they went up and explored the land from the Desert of Zin as far as Rehob, toward Lebo Hamath. They went up through the Negev and came to Hebron, where Ahiman, Sheshai and Talmai, the descendants of Anak, lived. (Hebron had been built seven years before Zoan in Egypt.) When they reached the Valley of Eshkol,[a] they cut off a branch bearing a single cluster of grapes. Two of them carried it on a pole between them, along with some pomegranates and figs. That place was called the Valley of Eshkol because of the cluster of grapes the Israelites cut off there. 25 At the end of forty days they returned from exploring the land.

They came back to Moses and Aaron and the whole Israelite community at Kadesh in the Desert of Paran. There they reported to them and to the whole assembly and showed them the fruit of the land. They gave Moses this account: "We went into the land to which you sent us, and it does flow with milk and honey! Here is its fruit. But the people who live there are powerful, and the cities are fortified and very large. We even saw descendants of Anak there. The Amalekites live in the Negev; the Hittites, Jebusites and Amorites live in the hill country; and the Canaanites live near the sea and along the Jordan."

Then Caleb silenced the people before Moses and said, "We should go up and take possession of the land, for we can certainly do it."

But the men who had gone up with him said, "We can't attack those people; they are stronger than we are." And they spread among the Israelites a bad report about the land they had explored.

They said, "The land we explored devours those living in it. All the people we saw there are of great size. We saw the Nephilim there (the descendants of Anak come from the Nephilim). We seemed like grasshoppers in our own eyes, and we looked the same to them."

Questions for Bible Reading Exercise Two

1. List seven things that Moses asked Israelites to do while exploring the land of Canaan.

   a. _____

   b. _____

   c. _____

   d. _____

   e. _____

   f. _____

   g. _____

2. What did they report to Moses and the people of Israel after returning from the land of Canaan?

   _____

   _____

   _____

   _____

3. Why were they afraid to possess the land?

4. What was Caleb's answer and admonishment?

5. What can you learn from Caleb's answer?

_____

_____

The Root Cause of Fear

Fear is caused by a deep sense of insecurity and a pessimistic interpretation of anticipated challenges. Most of it has to do with our imagination. Our thoughts begin to amplify and exaggerate the obstacles that stand in our way. That's why the more you focus on your obstacles the more your fear will cause you to become powerless. In the case of those Israelites to whom Moses delegated the responsibility of exploring the land, they did not focus their attention on the blessings of the land, but on the strength and power of their enemies. Faith, on the other hand, causes you to lean on God's power and His authority to help you win the battles of your life. Faith allows you to move forward with the solid confidence that God is bigger than all your enemies as well as all of your problems and challenges.

The Destructive Power of Fear

Fear blinds the mind to God's promises. Remember that God had already given the land of Canaan to the Israelites even before Moses sent those men out to explore it. It was already their land by faith. But, their fear caused them to forget that God had already given it to them. That's what fear does; it blinds the mind to God's promises. In this sense, fear can be the greatest blessings destroyer. When you have a strong conviction that a blessing belongs to you by faith, you don't worry about the challenges, you just move on. You will be amazed to witness how those challenges will disappear as move on to possess your inheritance.

Fear paralyzes our potentials. God had already equipped His people with everything necessary to possess the land. The entire angelic army was with them; they had the Red Sea experience in their resume; they had a vital proof of the manifestation of God's power, but fear caused them to feel ill-equipped to possess the land of Canaan. Fear can paralyze your potentials if you allow it to influence your thoughts and action. It can even cause you to act contrary to the word of God, causing you to drown like Peter: *Then Peter got down out of the boat, walked on the water and came toward Jesus. But when he saw the wind, he was afraid and, beginning to sink, cried out, "Lord, save me!"*

Immediately Jesus reached out his hand and caught him. "You of little faith," he said, "why did you doubt?"

Fear causes you to lack courage to stand up for what's right. That's what happened to Pilate in his decision-making process. He feared the crowd instead of realizing that his decision should been based on what is right, not what the angry and ill-motivated crowd wants. Read the following Scriptures and see how fear creates a lack of courage that will always lead to poor decisions.

Meanwhile Jesus stood before the governor, and the governor asked him, "Are you the king of the Jews?"

"You have said so," Jesus replied.

When he was accused by the chief priests and the elders, he gave no answer. Then Pilate asked him, "Don't you hear the testimony they are bringing against you?" But Jesus made no reply, not even to a single charge – to the great amazement of the governor.

Now it was the governor's custom at the festival to release a prisoner chosen by the crowd. At that time they had a well-known prisoner whose name was Jesus Barabbas. So when the crowd had gathered, Pilate asked them, "Which one do you want me to release to you: Jesus Barabbas, or Jesus who is called the Messiah?" For he knew it was out of self-interest that they had handed Jesus over to him. While Pilate was sitting on the judge's seat, his wife sent him this message: "Don't have anything to do with that innocent man, for I have suffered a great deal today in a dream because of him."

But the chief priests and the elders persuaded the crowd to ask for Barabbas and to have Jesus executed. Matthew 27:11-20.

Let us pray for faith, courage and strength in order to avoid cowardice in our decision-making process like Pilate. Being cowardly will kill our motivation to move forward and possess our inheritance in God. Let us follow Caleb's admonishment instead:

Then Caleb silenced the people before Moses and said, we should go up and take possession of the land, for we can certainly do it.

You certainly can do it if you allow the Holy Spirit to help you get rid of all your fears:

- Fear of failure
- Fear of deception
- Fear of ridicule from others
- Fear of rejection
- Fear of losing your grip
- Fear of your enemies
- Fear of the unknown

Whatever your fears may be, you may rest assured that through faith and action, God can empower you to completely get rid of them in order for you to possess your "Canaan land."

People often ask why chickens don't fly. The answer lies mainly in the word: fear. It can paralyze our possibilities for life. It makes you afraid to exercise your talents in order to develop them. Like chickens, we just maintain our daily routines without exploring the endless possibilities that God has made accessible to us.

Most of what we fear is only in our imagination. We just imagine a danger, and we allow it to be a solid reason for not moving forward.

Ask people what they fear the most in life, they may tell you failure. "If I start this ministry, I may fail." "If I pursue my education, I may not graduate." "If I get married, I may fail." "If I open a business, I may fail." Notice that most of it is just a mere illusion. You're afraid of something that you have not even tried yet. How can you presume that you will fail at something, if you never try it?

How do you overcome the fear of failure? You may do so by putting your belief and faith into action. Afterward, you will find out there was really nothing to be afraid of. You were just paralyzed by the fear of the unknown, which convinced you that you will fail if you try.

Another efficient way to overcome fear is to practice doing what you are afraid to do. If it's a good thing, why be afraid? The only fear you should have is the fear of not trying.

The only thing you should fear "is fear itself," because it can paralyze you mentally and physically. It can cause you to live a life full of regrets.

When you finally realize how much you could have accomplished were it not for the fear of failure, regrets will follow. Notice what Jesus said: *"Why are you so fearful, O ye of little faith."* Jesus places a great deal of emphasis on the word faith, because He knew that faith is the only thing that can drive fear completely out of your life. Faith is the exact opposite of fear. When you have fear, you lose your faith; but, when you have faith, you lose your fear.

> Fear cannot move any mountain, but faith will.

Fear cannot move any mountain, but faith will. Notice what Jesus told His disciples: *"Truly I tell you, if you have faith as small as a mustard seed, you can say to this mountain, 'Move from here to there,' and it will move. Nothing will be impossible for you."* Matthew 17:20.

Points worth special attention

- Practice looking up to God for your answers. Know that with God everything is possible.

- Rely on your faith and start doing the good things that you've always been afraid to do. You will soon realize that the biggest failure is the failure to try.
- Remind yourself daily that you have God-given talents (and you do!) and make an effort to start using them gradually until you overcome the fear of failure.
- Ask yourself this question: "How do I know I will fail at anything I try, if I don't try anything?"

Notes

Chapter 4:

Restoring Life's Vessel

We all know that God uses ordinary people who are solution oriented. That's why God compares himself to a patient and loving potter, and those people to the clay. In other words, when we place our lives completely in God's hands, He fashions us and molds us patiently in order to use us efficiently for the advancement of His kingdom on Earth. As you pick up a piece of clay, it looks like it does not have any value at all. But, as far as God is concerned, He is more interested in what He is able to do with the clay than the worthiness of the clay. In fact, the more marred the clay is, the more He enjoys remaking it for His glory to shine through it.

God knows us better than anybody, because He created us. There is nothing, absolutely nothing we may say to God about ourselves that will shock Him. He is the potter, we are the clay. He is able to do whatever He desires with His clay, because, of course, He is the potter. We read the following details about the various uses of clay from "Practical Primitive", a website by Eddie Starnater and Junie Martin:

Today we usually think of clay as being used for pottery, but in truth the uses are almost endless. For thousands of years man has used this substance for a whole host of things, from pigments to medicines.

As one of the most abundant materials on Earth, clay can be found almost anywhere — just look for areas where the ground has broken into a bark like pattern (as on a tree) or areas where water tends sit longer after a heavy rain.

Clay can be extracted from many of these sources quite easily, and whether you plan to use it for pottery or one of the numerous other traditional uses, the goal is to remove as many impurities as possible and the process is the same. While some clay deposits are pure enough to be used raw straight out of the ground, these are the exception; most clay is found in conjunction with sand.

The potter enjoys working with clay because the uses are endless. Clay is one of the most abundant materials on Earth, and it can be found anywhere. When working with clay, the goal is to remove as many impurities as possible in order to turn it into a great and useful vessel.

Let us study the various uses as mentioned above. This will help us to understand why God enjoys using ordinary people for the advancement of His kingdom.

The uses of clay are endless. This explains why the Bible uses the clay illustration to demonstrate how God uses ordinary people from all walks of life to accomplish great things according to His purpose on Earth. Clay is a naturally humble material that is found in conjunction with sand. It is synonymous with dirt. In fact, it is dirt. What amazes us is that God, the potter, enjoys working with the clay patiently, and when He is done with it, instead of the original insignificant piece of dirt, we see a masterpiece. There is no limit to what God can do with the clay in His hands; allow Him to use you, and you will rejoice in the fact that He can accomplish so much with so little. That's what He specializes in.

Clay is one of the most abundant materials on Earth. It can be found anywhere. It is very accessible. People don't even pay attention to it when they see it, because dirt is dirt. However, the potter loves and respects clay, because that's where his passion is. He loves and admires the clay. People may not see any potential in you; but your creator knows what he has invested in you. There is a seed of greatness in you that no one can see but your maker. Your existence here on Earth is not a mere accident. That's why you should never judge yourself according to what others think about you. You should always know that God knows you better than even your own self. You don't need to have a glorious background in order for Him to use you miraculously.

> There is a seed of greatness in you that no one can see but your maker.

Remember, God uses ordinary people. Here's what Paul said:

It does not, therefore, depend on human desire or effort, but on God's mercy. For Scripture says to Pharaoh: "I raised you up for this very purpose, that I might display my power in you and that my name might be proclaimed in all the earth." Therefore God has mercy on whom he wants to have mercy, and he hardens whom he wants to harden. One of you will say to me: "Then why does God still blame us? For who is God? Shall what is formed say to the one who formed it, 'Why did you make me like this?' Does not the potter have the right to make out of the same lump of clay some pottery for special purposes and some for common use? Romans 9:16–21.

The potter has earned the right to use the clay anyway He chooses to. He is the maker and designer with the master plan to create the pottery from the humble clay. Instead of complaining about what you don't have, learn to praise God for everything that He has done in your life thus far. He is not done with you yet. Trust Him to continue shaping you according to His purpose for your life. Here's what Jeremiah said:

For I know the plans I have for you," declares the LORD, "plans to prosper you and not to harm you, plans to give you hope and a future. Then you will call on me and come and pray to me, and I will listen to you. You will seek me and find me when you seek me with all your heart. I will be found by you," declares the LORD. Jeremiah 29:11-12.

Clay can be found anywhere. Have you ever wondered why clay is so accessible? I think, perhaps, it is God's way of reminding us that He is the potter behind every human master piece on Earth. It is His mercy that sustains us. We should always remember to give Him credit for our accomplishments. That's the primary reason for which He chooses to use ordinary people. As we take a closer look at where we came from, and where we are, we should be humble enough to admit it's God goodness that has been showering our lives. We should always have some valuable reasons to praise His Holy name. By giving Him the honor and credit for what He has done, He will certainly to do for us above and beyond what we would never anticipate.

When working with clay, the goal is to remove as many impurities as possible. Here is the potter's method of eliminating any unnecessary dirt from the clay. The clay must first be washed to remove the exterior dirt, mire and surface impurities. This initial washing will not be the last time the potter will use water to aid the process. We may compare the natural water of the potter to be a representation of our spiritual water which is the

Word of God. The Bible has this to say:

This is the word that came to Jeremiah from the LORD: "Go down to the potter's house, and there I will give you my message." So I went down to the potter's house, and I saw him working at the wheel.

But the pot he was shaping from the clay was marred in his hands; so the potter formed it into another pot, shaping it as seemed best to him.

Then the word of the LORD came to me: "O house of Israel, can I not do with you as this potter does?" declares the LORD. "Like clay in the hand of the potter, so are you in my hand, O house of Israel." Jeremiah 18:1-6.

Submit Your Vessel for Restoration

This process involves allowing God to purify us of anything that is contrary to His will, or anything that may cause us major setbacks on the plans that He wants to fulfill for our blessings.

Today, let us allow God to purify us, shape us, and use us for His glory. He can only do that if we allow Him to purge us from anything that is against His will. We must be willing to make room for the indwelling of His Holy Spirit. As someone has suggested before, *If you take a sponge and submerge it in a bucket of water, it will become saturated.* Saturated means it can't take any more water. Running a tap over it, dropping it in a swimming pool, tossing it in the river, won't make a difference - it's got as much water as it can take. Here's the thing: If you want that sponge to be able to take in extra water, what must you do? Wring it out. Obedience is like wringing out that sponge and the water is the Holy Spirit. That's why in order for God to restore us and shape us according to His will we must be willing for Him to wring out of us anything that may hinder our progress. The following is a long list of things that we must be wringed out of us in order for the power of God to manifest in our lives: Anger, anxiety, self-pity, regret, negative thinking, negative attitude, doubt, worry, hate, chronic frustration, pessimism, etc. By allowing the potter to change us, He will restore our vessels miraculously, and we will be able to serve Him successfully within the realm of our purpose.

> Today, let us allow God to purify us, shape us, and use us for His glory.

God uses several comparisons in the Bible to ensure that we truly understand the process and prepare for it. As you proceed with the following Bible Reading Exercise, reflect on various impacts it can generate depending on the type of ground it falls on.

Bible Reading Exercise One

The sower, the seed, and the soil

Matthew 13:16–40

But blessed are your eyes because they see, and your ears because they hear. For truly I tell you, many prophets and righteous people longed to see what you see but did not see it, and to hear what you hear but did not hear it.

"Listen then to what the parable of the sower means: When anyone hears the message about the kingdom and does not understand it, the evil one comes and snatches away what was sown in their heart. This is the seed sown along the path. The seed falling on rocky ground refers to someone who hears the word and at once receives it with joy. But since they have no root, they last only a short time. When trouble or persecution comes because of the word, they quickly fall away. The seed falling among the thorns refers to someone who hears the word, but the worries of this life and the deceitfulness of wealth choke the word, making it unfruitful. But the seed falling on good soil refers to someone who hears the word and understands it. This is the one who produces a crop, yielding a hundred, sixty or thirty times what was sown.

Questions for Bible Reading Exercise One

1. What is the main point of the parable of the sower?

_____

_____

_____

_____

_____

2. What does the evil one do when someone hears the message of the kingdom and does not understand?

_____

_____

_____

_____

_____

3. What happens when the seed of the word of God falls on rocky ground?

_____

_____

_____

_____

_____

_____

4. What happens when the seed of the word of God falls among thorns?

_____

_____

_____

_____

_____

5. What should you do in order for the seed of the word of God to be fruitful in your life?

_____

_____

_____

_____

_____

Bible Reading Exercise Two

The woman, the leaven, and the meal

Luke 13:18–21 – Then Jesus asked, "What is the kingdom of God like? What shall I compare it to? It is like a mustard seed, which a man took and planted in his garden. It grew and became a *tree, and the birds perched in its branches."*

Again he asked, "What shall I compare the kingdom of God to? It is like yeast that a woman took and mixed into about sixty pounds of flour until it worked all through the dough."

Questions for Bible Reading Exercise Two

1. Why did Jesus compare the kingdom of God with a mustard seed twice in two different verses?

_____

_____

_____

_____

_____

2. How does it apply to you as a kingdom-minded Christian aspiring to be used by God?

_____

_____

_____

_____

_____

3. Why does God expect kingdom-minded Christians to think big?

_____

_____

_____

_____

_____

Bible Reading Exercise Three

The vineyardist, the vineyard, and the fruit

Matthew 21:33–45 – 33 - Listen to another parable: There was a landowner who planted a vineyard. He put a wall around it, dug a winepress in it and built a watchtower. Then he rented the vineyard to some farmers and moved to another place. When the harvest time approached, he sent his servants to the tenants to collect his fruit.

"The tenants seized his servants; they beat one, killed another, and stoned a third. Then he sent other servants to them, more than the first time, and the tenants treated them the same way. Last of all, he sent his son to them. "They will respect my son," he said.

But when the tenants saw the son, they said to each other, "This is the heir. Come, let's kill him and take his inheritance." So they took him and threw him out of the vineyard and killed him.

Therefore, when the owner of the vineyard comes, what will he do to those tenants?

"He will bring those wretches to a wretched end," they replied, "and he will rent the vineyard to other tenants, who will give him his share of the crop at harvest time." Jesus said to them, "Have you never read in the Scriptures: "'The stone the builders rejected has become the cornerstone; the Lord has done this, and it is marvelous in our eyes'[h]?

"Therefore I tell you that the kingdom of God will be taken away from you and given to a people who will produce its fruit. Anyone who falls on this stone will be broken to pieces; anyone on whom it falls will be crushed."

Questions for Bible Reading Exercise Three

1. How does this parable relate to Christians who are not fruitful?

_____

_____

_____

_____

_____

2. Why did Jesus say: "The kingdom of God will be taken away from you and given to a people who will produce its fruits?" Explain in your own words what you can do to avoid the kingdom of God being taken away from you.

_____

_____

_____

_____

3. As clay in the potter's hands, what can you do to allow him to shape and mold you according to the promises of His Holy Word? Take a moment to think about your answer to this question before you write it down.

_____

_____

_____

_____

_____

The parables above focus mainly on the importance of God's word and the impact it makes on those who choose to obey it. They also focus on the consequences awaiting those who choose to disobey it. God has chosen to use the simile of a potter to show us that our life is not an accident, but a special design in His hand. He is able to transform our lives through the power of His word and the Holy Spirit. However, He can only do that when

His word falls on fertile ground. Take a moment now to allow His word to penetrate your heart.

When believers experience setbacks in their walk with God, many tend to lose hope and return to the world, when the right thing to do should be to place the clay in the potter's hands. Our God is so merciful that He takes great pleasure in rebuilding our lives for the glory of His everlasting kingdom. As marred vessels in God's merciful hands, we should always refer to His word in order to reaffirm our faith and dedication, and God would be more than willing to restore no matter how marred our vessels are. In the book of Lamentations, chapter 4:1–5, God extended an invitation for His people to return to Him for restoration.

> *How the gold has lost its luster,*
> *the fine gold become dull!*
> *The sacred gems are scattered*
> *at every street corner.*
> *How the precious children of Zion,*
> *once worth their weight in gold,*
> *are now considered as pots of clay,*
> *the work of a potter's hands!*
> *Even jackals offer their breasts*
> *to nurse their young,*

but my people have become heartless

like ostriches in the desert.

Because of thirst the infant's tongue

sticks to the roof of its mouth;

the children beg for bread,

but no one gives it to them.

Those who once ate delicacies

are destitute in the streets.

Those brought up in royal purple

now lie on ash heap. – Jeremiah 4:1–5

Just imagine how many people who once knew God are now living like marred vessels. How do you tell them there is hope? How do you share the admonishments of God's word with them? How do you encourage them to return to God?

Today, I encourage you to start creating time in your busy schedule to share the promises of God with those who are in need of it. When you understand that the Lord blesses you in order for you to bless others, you will be more determined than ever to touch others as He continues to touch you. So, practice seeing yourself as a workmanship of the great potter inviting others to that same source. The difference this acknowledgement will make in your life should influence every aspect of your daily endeavors. Other broken vessels will be restored because of your personal touch. Notice what Job said:

I am the same as you in God's sight;

I too am a piece of clay.

No fear of me should alarm you,

nor should my hand be heavy on you. – Job 33:6–7

As you seek to master these principles, try to teach them to anybody God sends your way. The more you teach them, the more you will assimilate and practice them for your own growth process.

While you are helping other people, you will be better equipped mentally to get rid of your own misconceptions that you grew up with about God and yourself. You will dissociate yourself from those misconceptions as you fully embrace who you really are.

You are not your past, you are not your unfortunate experiences; you are not even your present conditions. You are a precious child of God full of tremendous potential. The Lord is waiting to use you for the advancement of His everlasting kingdom.

Sometimes, friends and relatives may tell you that the reason why they could not accomplish much in life was because of some kind of misfortune, like a baby out of wedlock, a physical ailment, a bad marriage, a terrible divorce, a sudden death in the family, the loss of a good job, discontinued education, depression, anxiety, accidents, messed up reputation, bad credit, and the list goes on. However, when you realize that none of these things above defines you as a child of the living and mighty God, you will then be able to detach from them mentally and allow God to manifest His power in you. The notion that God is the potter and you are the clay will allow your dependence on God's power to be so strong that your problems will not affect you the same way they once did. You will see them with a different frame of mind.

Whatever you experience in your new journey now should serve as a bridge to cross over toward your destiny. At this level, your experiences in life will become your practical teachers. Instead of complaining about them, you will praise God for them like the psalmist did:

I waited patiently for the LORD;
he turned to me and heard my cry.
He lifted me out of the slimy pit,
out of the mud and mire;
he set my feet on a rock
and gave me a firm place to stand.

He put a new song in my mouth,

a hymn of praise to our God. – Psalm 40:2–3

Clay left to itself is helpless. It is utterly unable to make anything out of itself, and so are we when we reject our potter and maker. Unless we place ourselves in God's unfailing hand, we'll be helpless. Notice what Isaiah said:

You turn things upside down,

as if the potter were thought to be like the clay!

Shall what is formed say to the one who formed it,

"You did not make me"?

Can the pot say to the potter,

"You know nothing"? – Isaiah 29:16

Yet you, LORD, are our Father.

We are the clay, you are the potter;

we are all the work of your hand.

Do not be angry beyond measure, LORD;

do not remember our sins forever.

Oh, look on us, we pray,

for we are all your people. – Isaiah 64:8,9

The potter is an artist in his own right. He is capable of using his own pattern in order to fashion his vessels. Unless the clay is obedient and willing, the potter will not be able to fashion it into the master piece vessel He intends to create out of it.

When the vessel becomes marred in the potter's hand, he fails to achieve his original design with the clay in spite of great skills and effort. This shows that we are free moral agents, and that we must cooperate with our Maker in order for Him to use us in a mighty way. This is simply because no amount of effort by Him can do anything with us without our will and cooperation. The expression used by the prophet to convey this idea is "marred vessel," which means an impaired or disfigured vessel. The point is, no matter how impaired or disfigured our vessel is, the potter is capable of restoring it only if we allow Him to. If we resist His miraculous and loving intervention, He will not force us to do so, because we are free moral agents. Ask yourself the following questions as you meditate on the revelation of the word of God above:

What did the potter do with the vessel that was marred? Did He condemn it? Did He curse it? Did He reject it? Or did He cast it away as a total failure unworthy of further effort? Not at all, He made it another vessel. This leads us to understand

> Accept God's forgiveness as you live with the assurance that you have been transformed

that no matter how marred we are, God will not cast us away as insignificant and hopeless. He will restore us and use us as powerful instruments under the influence of the Holy Spirit.

Now that you've seen how God specializes in working over marred lives, take a moment to reflect on the areas of your life that need His infinite touch and power. As you willingly yield to Him, He will intervene in order to restore you in accordance with His promises.

Points worth special attention

- Consider yourself as the clay, and God as the potter, as you place your life and dreams in His unfailing hands. This means that you're willing to trust Him even for the most impossible solutions in your life.
- Make a conscious effort to share your faith with others. This will help you enhance your own spiritual growth process. Remember, the more you give, the more you receive. It is a basic given principle that may apply to just about any situation.
- Praise God every single day for the new you. Thank Him for making you a better person with greater and clearer vision. Thank Him for allowing you to realize your purpose

for being here on Earth. You need to do this even in times of setbacks and difficulties. Praising and thanking God while experiencing tough times will tell your enemies that you intend to fight your battles until you die. They will understand that you're focused and determined. Trying to discourage you won't work.

- Accept God's forgiveness as you live with the assurance that you have been transformed. This will open the door widely for you to become confident and solution oriented instead of being guilty and confused. Many believers still maintain a guilty feeling even after God has forgiven them. Guilt will cause fear to overtake your life. When you pray for forgiveness, you must accept it by faith. You will feel refreshed and reenergized spiritually.

Notes

_____

_____

_____

_____

_____

Chapter 5:

Flying Above Life's Financial Hurdles

Without Godly people who have a vision for God's purposes, who have a heart to obey God and who have proven integrity with finances, we cannot expect God to release large amounts of wealth.

— Peter Wagner

Among the varied excellent qualities of a Christian is the ability of adoption and adjustment to all circumstances and conditions in this life. Paul understood this very well. Here's what he said:

I rejoiced greatly in the Lord that at last you renewed your concern for me. Indeed, you were concerned, but you had no opportunity to show it. I am not saying this because I am in need, for I have learned to be content whatever the circumstances. I know what it is to be in need, and I know what it is to have plenty. I have learned the secret of being content in any and every situation, whether well fed or hungry, whether living in plenty or in want. I can do all this through him who gives me strength. Philippians 4:10–13.

As far as Paul is concerned, Christians should be able to adapt and adjust to all circumstances and conditions in this life. That's why when they become rich they are able to provide financial support for the advancement of God's kingdom. They are able to manage their wealth instead of their wealth managing them. They are very much aware that while prosperity paves the way for so many blessings, it can become dangerous to those who can't handle it appropriately.

Prosperity is not just about accumulating wealth, it is about managing it in a Godly way so that we may grow in grace and become useful tools in God's hand. We all appreciate wealthy Christians who maintain their spirituality and usefulness in the support of the Gospel of Jesus Christ. We often like to praise God for their faithfulness, which is an excellent thing to do. But, the question we often ask is why does God bless them with so much wealth? We fail to realize that their biggest blessing is not the wealth itself, but their intimate relationship with God. As a result, God blesses their abilities and talents, knowing that, as they become wealthy, they will not abandon their Godly heritage. Their spirituality will not be shaken by what they possess. And, Instead of the world influencing them, they influence the world for Christ. They do not hesitate to provide financial support to God's Church, because they are persuaded, it's the greatest investment on Earth. No other investment can yield a greater return. That's an indication of the reason why God's power is demonstrated in everything they do. What God has done for those wealthy Christians is very much similar to what He has done for Joseph:

> *The LORD was with Joseph so that he prospered, and he lived in the house of his Egyptian master. When his master saw that the LORD was with him and that the LORD gave him success in everything he did, Joseph found favor in his eyes and became his attendant. Potiphar put him in charge of his household, and he entrusted to his care everything he owned. From the time he put him in charge of his household and of all that he owned, the LORD blessed the household of the Egyptian because of Joseph. The blessing of the LORD was on everything Potiphar had, both in the house and in the field. So Potiphar left everything he had in Joseph's care; with Joseph in charge, he did not concern himself with anything except the food he ate.* Genesis 39:1–6.

Trust is a major component of the wealth entrusted to believers. God enjoys promoting His people from lesser to greater responsibility because of the high level of trust involved both ways. They trust God and God trusts them as well. You can see, thus far, that trust is a major component of the prosperity entrusted to believers in the kingdom of God. It has to do with how much you trust God and how much God trusts you. The stronger the trusting bond, the more you can expect God to bless you with.

Competency is an essential element for true prosperity. There must be a measure of competency. By that I mean, you must have developed the skills required to handle the wealth in a way that is efficient and consistent with the will of God. You must be able to reap a maximum result in the way you manage and invest what God entrusts to you. That measure of competency must be demonstrated in everything that you do as a kingdom-minded believer. If not, prosperity would be a danger instead of a blessing. Competency in any area of expertise allows you to use your skills efficiently in order for your mind to expand positively on the tasks ahead of us. As believers, we get our primary inspiration and motivation from our creator. That's why we are able to experience peace of mind even in the midst of chaotic situations. Those who don't get their primary inspiration and motivation from God risk being confused and miserable in spite of their wealth. Let us reflect on some biblical examples.

> You cannot inherit the kingdom of God if you lack a sincere relationship with Him

Nadal – a man who was wealthy but foolish

A certain man in Maon, who had property there at Carmel, was very wealthy. He had a thousand goats and three thousand sheep, which he was shearing in Carmel. His name was Nabal and his wife's name was Abigail. She was an intelligent and beautiful woman, but her husband was surly and mean in his dealings – he was a Calebite. 1 Samuel 25:2.

The rich young ruler – he was wealthy but lacked wisdom
Five lessons Jesus intended to teach us from this story.

1. Jesus did not say that the rich will not inherit the kingdom of God. He simply meant that it's harder for a rich man who is in love with money to inherit the kingdom of God, because "the love of money is the root of all evil."

2. Jesus meant that only those who are kingdom-minded will inherit the kingdom.

3. His core message was: if your wealth is more important to you than the kingdom of God, you will not be able to enter. No matter how important money is, it cannot save anyone, only Jesus can.

4. It's almost impossible to save someone whose heart is not on the things of God. That's the meaning of the camel's illustration.

5. You cannot inherit the kingdom of God if you lack a sincere relationship with Him.

    As you carefully read the story below, try to depict several reasons why it is harder for some (not all) wealthy people to inherit the kingdom of God.

Just then a man came up to Jesus and asked, "Teacher, what good thing must I do to get eternal life?"

"Why do you ask me about what is good?" Jesus replied. "There is only One who is good. If you want to enter life, keep the commandments."

"Which ones?" he inquired.

Jesus replied, "'You shall not murder, you shall not commit adultery, you shall not steal, you shall not give false testimony, honor your father and mother, and 'love your neighbor as yourself.'

"All these I have kept," the young man said. "What do I still lack?"

Jesus answered, "If you want to be perfect, go, sell your possessions and give to the poor, and you will have treasure in heaven. Then come, follow me."

When the young man heard this, he went away sad, because he had great wealth.

Then Jesus said to his disciples, "Truly I tell you, it is hard for someone who is rich to enter the kingdom of heaven. Again I tell you, it is easier for a camel to go through the eye of a needle than for someone who is rich to enter the kingdom of God."

When the disciples heard this, they were greatly astonished and asked, "Who then can be saved?"

Jesus looked at them and said, "With man this is impossible, but with God all things are possible."

Reason Number One

_____

_____

_____

_____

Reason Number Two

_____

_____

_____

_____

Reason Number Three

_____

_____

_____

_____

The rich young ruler had money and fame but lacked the wisdom of the kingdom. He failed every single one of the tests

Jesus performed on Him. As you might have already depicted from your own reflection on the story, he lacks the very thing that would help him live a balance Christian life. Many become wealthy in the world, but without divine wisdom, they are forced to live a miserable life. They cannot afford to really enjoy their wealth. Here's what Solomon said:

Wisdom, like an inheritance, is a good thing

and benefits those who see the sun.

Wisdom is a shelter

as money is a shelter,

but the advantage of knowledge is this:

Wisdom preserves those who have it. Ecclesiastes 7:11,12

Wisdom preserves those who have it. Wisdom is what will preserve you as you prosper in life. How does wisdom preserve those who have it? As we think about it, wisdom is what keeps us moving in the right direction. Without it, our mistakes and setbacks would multiply daily to a level where we would not be able to maintain control of what we do. You imagine being wealthy without the wisdom of God. You imagine being wealthy without the power of God as the motivating factor in your life. It would be nearly impossible to even enjoy what you have. What wisdom does, it allows you to wake up every single day with the right agenda and focus so that you don't function like a robot. It allows you to fly with the right perspectives and motives in order for your wealth to be used appropriately and productively. When it's done this way, the money benefits everyone and everything in need of it. God's kingdom on Earth is made accessible to everyone seeking to know Him better in order to serve Him. Believe it or not, money plays a major role in the preaching of the Gospel of Jesus Christ by providing the means necessary to carry the truth to people all around the world. Without money, the preaching of the Gospel would be very limited. That's why, in order for God to entrust His wealth to you as a believer, He has to make sure that you will use it for the right cause, at the right time, in the right place. This is what I call money spent wisely, because it has not been wasted in the vain pleasures of this world. It has been used for the right cause and purpose leaving you with a feeling of satisfaction knowing, with God's help, you have done the right thing.

ced*Wisdom, like inheritance, is a good thing and benefits those who see the sun.* How does wisdom benefit those who see the sun? As a wealthy believer, wisdom benefits you, because it helps you maintain your relationship with the Lord while managing the riches He has placed in your hands. Remember,

God cannot entrust His wealth to everyone. He has to be certain it will not stand as a stumbling block in the way of your salvation. Otherwise, you would give more importance to your possessions than the one who gives you those possessions. Wisdom opens your eyes widely in order to help you see the difference. Many wealthy people are confused and perplexed, because they can't see the difference between the two. Instead of God being the center of their lives, money is. In this case, money can cause you to make the wrong decisions for your life. Money can cause you to seek happiness from the wrong things in this life, leaving you confused, dissatisfied, and discouraged. This explains, in part, why the suicide rate is so high among some classes of wealthy individuals.

> Wisdom, like inheritance, is a good thing and benefits those who see the sun

Wealth is hard and almost impossible to handle without God's wisdom. That's why the Bible says: *Wisdom, like inheritance, is a good thing and benefits those who see the sun.* While you pray for wisdom, remember to maintain an attitude of praise toward God for bestowing His blessings upon your life. Practice thanking Him for Favor. By doing so, it will become easier for you to realize that He is the giver and you are the receiver. In the midst of abundance and prosperity, the giver needs to be praised, not the receiver. Always remember that.

Wealthy Christians should cultivate an attitude of praise and honor to God in the midst of their abundance and prosperity. When we become prosperous, we may be tempted to forget God. We may be tempted to forget that He is the one who paved the way for our success and prosperity. That's why we need to erect a solid fence around our relationship with God that will help us to maintain a humble spirit and a heart full of praise and gratitude. Remember, your relationship with your Savior is more important than anything you will ever possess. By keeping an attitude of praise toward God daily, you will be reminded constantly that God is the source of your wealth not you. Praise Him for every enjoyment within your financial realm both privately and publicly. Read how David, one of the wealthiest men who ever lived, cultivated a spirit of praise and gratitude toward God for blessing him with so much wealth. He did it privately and publicly.

David praised the LORD in the presence of the whole assembly,

saying,

"Praise be to you, LORD,

the God of our father Israel,

from everlasting to everlasting.

Yours, LORD, is the greatness and the power

and the glory and the majesty and the splendor,

for everything in heaven and earth is yours.

Yours, LORD, is the kingdom;

you are exalted as head over all.

Wealth and honor come from you;

you are the ruler of all things.

In your hands are strength and power

to exalt and give strength to all.

Now, our God, we give you thanks,

and praise your glorious name.

But who am I, and who are my people, that we should be able to give as generously as this? Everything comes from you, and we have given you only what comes from your hand. We are foreigners and strangers in your sight, as were all our ancestors. Our days on earth are like a shadow, without hope. LORD our God, all this abundance that we have provided for building you a temple for your Holy Name comes from your hand, and all of it belongs to you. I know, my God, that you test the heart and are pleased with integrity. All these things I have given willingly and with honest intent. And now I have seen with joy how willingly your people who are here have given to you. LORD, the God of our fathers Abraham, Isaac and Israel, keep these desires and thoughts in the hearts of your people forever, and keep their hearts loyal to you. 1 Chronicles 29:11–17.

Remember, like David, to cultivate a spirit of praise and gratitude to God for blessing you with so much wealth. Not only is He going to continue blessing you, He will continue to provide you with the wisdom and peace of mind necessary to manage your wealth wisely in accordance with His will and purpose.

For Solomon, wealth was a disaster that caused Him to lose his wisdom and his relationship with God. Here's what he had to ask of God toward the end of his life:

Two things I ask of you, LORD;

do not refuse me before I die:

Keep falsehood and lies far from me;

give me neither poverty nor riches,

but give me only my daily bread.

Otherwise, I may have too much and disown you

and say, 'Who is the LORD?'

Or I may become poor and steal,

and so dishonor the name of my God."

That should help us understand why the psalmist said: *If riches increase, set not your heart upon them.* Psalm 62:10.

Solomon later said: *He that trusts in his riches shall fall.* Proverbs 11:28.

When you fail to remember the source of your riches; when you fail to give credit to whom it is due, expect your wealth to pave the way for disaster and downfall in your life. That's why it is vitally important to erect a spiritual fence around your relationship with God on a daily basis in order to avoid worldliness or conformity to the world. John and James warned against such worldliness.

Do not love the world or anything in the world. If anyone loves the world, love for the Father[d] is not in them. For everything in the world—the lust of the flesh, the lust of the eyes, and the pride of life—comes not from the Father but from the world. The world and its desires pass away, but whoever does the will of God lives forever. 1 John 2:15–17.

Now listen, you rich people, weep and wail because of the misery that is coming on you. Your wealth has rotted, and moths have eaten your clothes. Your gold and silver are corroded. Their corrosion will testify against you and eat your flesh like fire. You have hoarded wealth in the last days. Look! The wages you failed to pay the workers who mowed your fields are crying out against you. The cries of the harvesters have reached the ears of the Lord

Almighty. You have lived on Earth in luxury and self-indulgence. You have fattened yourselves in the day of slaughter. You have condemned and murdered the innocent one, who was not opposing you. James 5:1–6.

Prosperity, in itself, is not evil; it is a blessing, if used rightly. Abraham was an excellent example as far as using wealth wisely. He was very wealthy, and God wanted it that way; but Lot, who also was wealthy, used his wealth the wrong way, and it turned against him. That's why if the Lord allows you to prosper, you should maintain a humble spirit; let us cultivate a spirit of praise and gratitude to our Lord who is the source of all blessings. Let us remember to use our wealth wisely to further the cause of His great kingdom on Earth. Let us remain faithful and obedient to Him in everything that we do. Without the shadow of a doubt, He will continue to bless us.

Points worth special attention

- God will not bless you with wealth until your heart is ready for it.
- God gives wealth for wise distribution in conformity with His purpose. It should not be kept for personal pride and greediness. Prosperity should not be about accumulating

wealth; It should be about managing and distributing wealth God's way so that we may grow in grace and become useful tools in God's hand.

- Before God entrusts wealth to you as a believer, He wants you to be certain that it will not stand as a stumbling block in the way of your salvation.
- In the midst of prosperity, the giver has to be praised, not the receiver.
- We must always remember to praise God from whom all blessings flow. His blessings should never be used for self-elevation, they should be an excellent opportunity for us to praise His name and majesty before all nations and tongues.
- Prosperity, in itself, is not evil. It is indeed a blessing if used rightly.

Chapter 6:

Healing Life's Damaged Wings

How many times in our life do we feel like a complete failure? How many times do we feel like throwing in the towel? How many times do we feel like giving up? How many times do we feel like there is nothing left in us to give? How many times do we talk ourselves down so low that it is nearly impossible to rise back up? The problems we cause to our own psyche in those moments may cause us to damage our own wings in such a way that we may lose our freedom to fly.

Damaged birds' wings sometimes may not be fully repaired in order to allow a stable and successful flight. They may continue to live the rest of their life without the ability to fly. Birds with damaged wings have to endure a painful process. They are sometimes forced to live in captivity. That's the risk we take when we allow our thoughts to dwell on anything that holds us in bondage, such as:

- ***"I've tried so many times, but I keep on failing over and over again."*** Let's thank God that you had the strength to try something several times. If you carefully reflect on it, you may come to the realization that you learned something new each time you tried. Whatever it was, you may consider it a step toward what you were trying to accomplish. Life is a classroom where we are constantly learning. Of course, not every lesson is easy; some may be harder than others, but the truth is you learned something new each time you try. In order to eliminate this thought pattern, you have to convince yourself each time: "I did not get exactly what I wanted, but at least, I've learned something new. I will use it as a useful tool next time." You will grow stronger and stronger until you develop the strength to fight through your challenges.

- *Life is unfair.* Each time you complain about that, you damage your wings. You force yourself to accept the erroneous idea that it is not necessary to progress, because progress is impossible. However, faith does the opposite; it teaches you that you control your destiny through the enabling power of the Holy Spirit. If you could reach the psyche of people who are discouraged, you would see that they damaged it themselves with self-defeating thoughts. They hold their hopes and dreams in the captivity of their negative thoughts. Each time you're tempted to say, "life is unfair," you may reverse it by saying something like: "Thank God I have power over my life! I choose not to allow this to discourage me." Keep saying this until it's fully registered and becomes almost automatic. This will help you to let go of the misconceptions that hinder your progress.

- *"I've been through so much, that I don't have any*

strength left in me." Birds with damaged wings live with the frustrating pain of not being able to fly anymore. When people reach this point, they are ready to give up all efforts. They may stop attending school; they may stop their motivation; they may even stop believing that they can do anything worthwhile. This stage is extremely frustrating emotionally. Humanly speaking, this can only happen to you when you allow it to happen. You own your emotional wings. That's why you should be careful not to damage them, or else, you will not be able to fly unless you allow God to renew your mind and heart for a fresh start.

> Allow God to renew your mind and heart for a fresh start

Be careful when you make statements like: "My past is too painful for me to be optimistic about my future." Or: "I came from a dysfunctional family, I don't think I can have a happy family." Or: "I've been hurt so many times. I can't afford to be hurt again."

While your past experiences may be painful, it doesn't help to use them as deciding factors for your motivation to move forward. It doesn't help to dwell on them. Remember, whatever you think about regularly will expand and become a focus point in your life. You really should not have to spend your energy on anything that can keep you in bondage. This is where you need to replace painful memories with good ones. With God's help you will be able to do that. He will help you reverse the process by the renewing of your mind; by making room for a new mentality. Notice what Paul said: "Be transformed by the renewing of your mind."

There are times when we may feel that even our best efforts are nothing but failures. The danger with those self-destructive feelings is that they may build in us a core belief system where we constantly hold ourselves down. I'm sure you've seen people who are so discouraged that they give up all hope.

Blaming everyone else is another extreme to avoid. Some people tend to blame everybody else for their misfortunes in life except themselves. It's like somebody else is responsible for every single problem they face until they convince themselves that they can't do anything about it. What they fail to realize is that life itself is a battlefield where we all need to fight our way through until we die. As believers, we are blessed to have full access to the divine powerhouse where we may claim our victory in spite of major hurdles. With a new mentality, God will help us not to focus on our past, but on what's ahead of us. Paul told us what to do in order to avoid damaging our own wings and fly toward the future:

One thing I do: Forgetting what is behind and straining toward what is ahead, I press on toward the goal to win the prize for which God has called me heavenward in Christ Jesus. – Philippians 3:13, 14.

If you could only measure the Lord's expectations for you as a faithful believer, you would have the faith to rejoice even in the face of your biggest challenges. You would pray daily for the Holy Spirit to empower you in order to experience a paradigm shift where your attention would shift from your past to your future. What we fail to understand, sometimes, is that our challenges are platforms for the greatest miracles of God on Earth. That's where He demonstrates to the whole world that He is God.

Why we sometimes see ourselves as failures

There are times when we project certain objectives for ourselves according to our own erroneous interpretation of success. When we strive and fail to reach those objectives, we think we have failed, but in reality, we have not. We simply have not met our expectations. If this ever happens to you, you should understand that you have not discovered your purpose yet. Your purpose allows you to take every challenge as an opportunity instead of a failure. Why not pray and ask God to help you discover your real purpose. In that case, every objective you project will fall in line with your purpose and will help you understand that what you call a failure is just another step toward the complete manifestation of your purpose.

Discouragement may also cause us to damage our own wings. While it is common for all of us to get discouraged, staying discouraged can be a major cause of damaged wings. The Bible gives us a whole range of examples where some women and men of God have gotten discouraged, but they did not remain discouraged.

> The three P's of spiritual and emotional restoration: Prayer, Praise, and Patience.

The psalmist David experienced a moment of discouragement in his life, which prompted him to damage his spiritual wings temporarily. Here's what the Bible says:

But David thought to himself, "One of these days I will be destroyed by the hand of Saul. The best thing I can do is to escape to the land of the Philistines. Then Saul will give up searching for me anywhere in Israel, and I will slip out of his hand. 1 Samuel 27:1

David was a brave warrior and a great king, but when the spirit of discouragement took hold of him, fear caused him to run away from Saul. If he remained discouraged, it would have been a major setback on everything that God called him to do. David, however, did manage to make a miraculous exit from his discouragement. Jonah is another example of discouragement that went deeper than that of David:

"Now, LORD, take away my life, for it is better for me to die than to live." But the LORD replied, "Is it right for you to be angry?"

Jonah had gone out and sat down at a place east of the city. There he made himself a shelter, sat in its shade and waited to see what would happen to the city. Then the LORD God provided a leafy plant and made it grow up over Jonah to give shade for his head to ease his discomfort, and Jonah was very happy about the plant. But at dawn the next day God provided a worm, which chewed the plant so that it withered. When the sun rose, God provided a scorching east wind, and the sun blazed on Jonah's head so that he grew faint. He wanted to die, and said, "It would be better for me to die than to live". – Jonah 4: 3-8

What does Jonah's experience reveal to you? I think it suggests that when you allow discouragement to overtake your life, you may come to the point where you even want to die. You only live for your disappointments, as you fail to realize that with God nothing is impossible.

Both David and Jonah were able to come to their senses

and place their worries in God's hands and He delivered them. They both came to realize that there is no such thing as failure. Apparent failures are, at time, blessings in disguise.

Many on Earth who thought they were a failure were the very ones who accomplished great and remarkable achievements in the world. Notice what they said before they discovered their greatness and influence.

- Calvin said to those who were with him before he died: "All that I have done is no value, and I am a miserable creature." Was all that he has done really of no value? Not at all.
- Cecil Rhodes said, after leaving his mark on the continent: "So little done, so much to do." Is this true? No, it's not.
- Abraham Lincoln, after his debate with Stephen Douglas, said his speech was a failure. Was his speech really a failure? Not at all. It was one of the greatest in history.

Paul was right when he said: *Therefore, my dear brothers and sisters, stand firm. Let nothing move you. Always give yourselves fully to the work of the Lord, because you know that your labor in the Lord is not in vain.* – 1 Corinthians 15:58.

Points worth special attention

Avoid negative self-talk that may cause you to get discouraged over your challenges.

- Learn to live your problem in God's hands.
- Remember that God specializes in things that are impossible.
- Avoid self-defeating thought patterns, such as saying: "I will never make it." Never say, "I am not smart enough," or "My past is too painful for me to overcome it." Don't say, "I can't anymore. I'm about to throw out the towel."

Those are self-defeating misconceptions that can cause you to damage your own wings. Once our spiritual wings have been self-damaged, the only way for us to survive is to allow God to change our mentality about God, ourselves and others. I think one of the best ways to start is through what I call the three P's of spiritual and emotional restoration: Prayer, Praise, and Patience.

- *Prayer* – Take time every day to bring your pains to the Lord in prayer. Best time to start is very early in the morning while everybody in the house is still asleep. Engage in a spiritual conversation just between you and the Lord. I mean, just talk to Him; open up your heart to Him until you strongly feel the connection.
- *Praise* – It's amazing what a spirit of praise and gratitude to God can do for us when the devil is trying to convince us that we're the most miserable people on Earth. We know he

is a liar. That's why we should focus our attention on God's goodness instead of our problems.

- **Patience** – Patience is not just a word; it is an excellent virtue that we should pray for every day. It allows us to wait patiently on God in spite of our challenges, knowing that God will reward us in due time.

Notes

_____

_____

_____

_____

_____

_____

_____

_____

_____

_____

_____

_____

_____

_____

Chapter 7:

Fertilizing Life's Spiritual Garden

Let us consider how plants benefit from fertilizers, since this may inspire us to fertilize our mind with the right ingredients.

Adding fertilizers at the initial planting and during the growing season ensures your plant will receive all the essential nutrients it needs for proper growth. You may compare this to the growing season in your relationship with God when your heart is open to the influence of the Holy Spirit. You experience this growth when you pray on a regular basis for the power of the Holy Spirit to influence your whole life. By doing so, you allow the Holy Spirit to take charge of everything that has to do with you.

In order to supplement a plant's life during growing season, a slow-release fertilizer may be added at the initial planting. Spiritually this implies that every believer should have a growing season in which they purposely schedule private time for Bible studies and spiritual growth. The best time to do this is early in the morning before you begin your activities. This allows you to fertilize your personal relationship with God on a daily basis.

Adding fertilizer to your plants will not only ensure the plants receive the proper amount of supplemental foods, it also ensures lush growth and beautiful flowers depending on the type of plant. On a spiritual level this means that believers should make sure they receive the proper amount of spiritual nourishment regularly in order to maintain a healthy relationship with the Lord. Over the years, I have developed the habit of collecting every piece of spiritual advice that God sends my way through books, sermons, Bible studies and songs. I add them as fertilizers to my spiritual plant to ensure that I receive the proper amount of supplemental spiritual foods necessary for my spiritual growth. This is vital because any plant that does not grow will eventually shrink and die. God uses those as supplemental means to nourish your spiritual life for growth and efficiency.

> Our root system as believers should be the word of God.

A plant can take in fertilizer through the soil by the root systems, or through the leaves during foliar feeding. Our root system as believers should be the word of God. It should be the principal spiritual fertilizer that fuels our relationship with our Lord.

It is best to add a slow-release fertilizer during the initial planting. A slow-release fertilizer has an internal timing system that only allows a certain amount of fertilizer chemicals to be absorbed at one time. By this you understand why the word of God encourages daily devotion instead of monthly or yearly devotion. It allows us to grow spiritually one day at a time. Every time in your busy life you miss your daily devotion, you skip a portion of your slow-release spiritual growth process.

The right fertilizer will improve the root systems and ensure your plant will have lush growth. When your relationship with God has a solid foundation in His word, you can serve Him with the assurance that your life will have lush growth in every profitable area. Without the determination to study the word of God and know it for yourself, you will not be able to experience that lush growth in your personal relationship with Him.

Fertilize your life with spirit-filled prayers

Spirit-filled and mountain-moving prayers indicate a stable relationship with the Lord, which allows you to cast out all your fears while your faith expands. David had this to say: *Yea, though I walk through the valley of the shadow of death, I fear no evil; for you are with me* – Psalm 23:4.

David knew the importance of prayers fertilized with the right ingredients. He was not concerned that the enemy of his soul would destroy him. We learn from David that our prayers must be highly personal; they must indicate a personal relationship with God; they must denote a sense of security; they must demonstrate earnestness and perseverance. – *O Lord God of my salvation... Let my prayer come before you, incline your ear unto my cry.* This prayer from David's heart suggests that we develop the habit of making our prayers more personalized and to the point.

We have a tendency to be so abundant in our prayers that we sometimes fail to include the essential ingredients. We fail to present our real personal needs. We think that God is some kind of spirit out there waiting for us to impress Him with our holiness, our knowledge of the Bible, and our oratorical skills. But, all we have to do is to open our hearts to Him as we would with our best friend.

Our Savior used His personal relation in the darkest hour of His earthly ministry:

From noon until three in the afternoon darkness came over all the land. About three in the afternoon Jesus cried out in a loud voice, "Eli, Eli, lema sabachthani?" (Which means "My God, my God, why have you forsaken me?") – Matthew 27:45,46.

Jesus was able to refer to His father as "My God" because the connection was already there. This implies that when you are in the darkest hour of your life, the only refuge that you can depend on is your personal relationship with God. It must be recognized, felt, and known even when you are facing difficulties and sufferings that are beyond explanation.

Instead of complaining about your suffering, you should see it as a test to your faith, because these tests will come over and over again as you mature in faith with God. Job, in spite of his horrible suffering, had the courage to say: *I know my redeemer lives – Job19:25.* Paul with his persecutions and thorn in the flesh had this assurance: *"For I know in whom I have believed – 2Tim 1:12.* The personalized relationship with the Lord brings a sense of peace to us that nothing else on the face of this Earth can bring.

It's not enough to feel that God is with you; it's not enough to think that God is with you – it's something you should just know. He hears you and feels you; He will help you overcome your trials and tribulations; your mountains will be removed; you can depend on Him; you can trust Him. Why? Because the personal relationship with the Lord is mainly about knowing Him and trusting Him no matter which side of life you're dealing with; no matter what scary mountains you're climbing.

I don't know of any men of God in the Bible who experienced the manifestation of the power of God on a personal level without knowing Him. They all were so close to Him that they knew Him not only as their God, but as their closest friend.

You need to build a solid relationship with Him that will keep you empowered even in times of hardships. You need to know Him for yourself. That's how you will be able to uphold your faith in Him in every situation. The writer of the book of Hebrews said this: *Without faith it is impossible to please God, because anyone who comes to him must believe that he exists and that he rewards those who earnestly seek him.* – Hebrews 11:6

A spiritually fertilized relationship provides a solid sense of security

Though I walk through the valley of the shadow of death, I will fear no evil because you are with me – Psalm 23:4. The personalized relationship with the Lord provides a sense of security that is based on the assurance that God is with you. Without that sense of security, it's impossible to have faith in God. What happens when you don't have it? Each time you experience a major crisis, fear and panic overshadow your faith, causing you to feel powerless and insecure. That's why it's always the will of God for you to feel secure. This sense of security is a vital proof that your faith is well grounded in your Savior. As we think about it, this was the secret of the three Hebrew young men:

Shadrach, Meshach and Abednego replied to him, "King Nebuchadnezzar, we do not need to defend ourselves before you in this matter. If we are thrown into the blazing furnace, the God we serve is able to deliver us from it, and he will deliver us from Your Majesty's hand. But even if he does not, we want you to know, Your Majesty, that we will not serve your gods. – Daniel 3:17-19.

Their sense of security was so remarkable that the threat of the king didn't scratch their faith. As a result, God honored their conviction and delivered them from the fiery furnace.

David had a similar experience in his challenge against Goliath:

He said to the Philistine, *You come against me with sword and spear and javelin, but I come against you in the name of the LORD Almighty, the God of the armies of Israel, whom you have defied. This day the LORD will deliver you into my hands, and I'll strike you down and cut off your head. This very day I will give the carcasses of the Philistine army to the birds and the wild animals, and the whole world will know that there is a God in Israel. All those gathered here will know that it is not by sword or spear that the LORD saves; for the battle is the LORD's, and he will give all of you into our hands.* – 1 Samuel 17:45-47.

That sense of security was so strong in David that the size and ammunitions of Goliath did not intimidate him. In fact, he assured Goliath that God would deliver him into his hands.

There was no trace of doubt or hesitation in any of David's words. You can understand why in every attack of the devil against us he tries to kill that sense of security in us. Without it we would not be able to resist him.

Earnestness and perseverance will nourish that sense of security – *O Lord God of my salvation, I have cried day and night before you; let my prayer come before you; incline your ear unto my cry.* Prayers that show earnestness and perseverance are motivated by urgent needs that only God is able to meet. Those needs are so urgent that they serve as a bridge to a stronger and more fervent relationship with God.

People who experience those moments of earnestness and perseverance in prayer will tell you that they often express their feelings of gratitude to the Lord for the experience. After overcoming those major hurdles, they have a closer and more purposeful walk with God. They become so immune to problems and difficulties, they no longer complain about them. For each occurrence, they just know it's another great mountain that God is about to remove. They know the blessings of earnestness and perseverance through personalized prayers. In the book of Deuteronomy, the Bible has this to say: *Your strength will equal your days* – Deuteronomy 33:25.

The strength that you develop while experiencing the hardships of your life will empower you to be the master of your destiny. When you reach this level of spiritual maturity, you will discover that problems don't bother you as much as they used to. You will not be concerned about routine in your prayer life; you will maintain a consistent spiritual companionship with God day and night. This type of earnestness and perseverance in prayer will equip you with everything you need physically, mentally, and spiritually to climb your mountain.

Points worth special attention

- Make personalized prayers a part of your daily devotion in order to reap the blessings of constant communion with the Great Problem Solver.
- Keep calm and peaceful in order for your mind to stay on God. Here's what David had to say: *You will keep calm and peaceful those whose minds are on you* – Isaiah 26:3.
- Seek to know God instead of feeling Him. When you know God is with you and cares for you, your soul will be at peace in every situation. *The Lord is my light and my salvation; whom shall I fear? The Lord is the strength of my life; of whom shall I be afraid?* – Psalm 27:1

- Allow your faith in God to instill in you a sense of security that leaves no room for doubt. You may even begin to thank God for your miracles before they happen. Pray for your miracles, claim them, and receive them by faith. Let us consider the words of Jesus on this point: *Then Jesus said, "Did I not tell you that if you believe, you will see the glory of God?" So they took away the stone. Then Jesus looked up and said, "Father, I thank you that you have heard me. I knew that you always hear me, but I said this for the benefit of the people standing here, that they may believe that you sent me." When he had said this, Jesus called in a loud voice, "Lazarus, come out!" The dead man came out, his hands and feet wrapped with strips of linen, and a cloth around his face. Jesus said to them, "Take off the grave clothes and let him go."* – John 11:40–42. Notice that the miracle did not happen yet when Jesus thanked His father for it. He asked for it, claimed it, and received it by faith.
- Learn to praise God for your answers even before you receive them. That's a great indication of faith in action.
- Remember that your personal relationship with God opens heaven wide and gives you free access to the storehouse of God's miracles.

- Your spiritual maturity and strength will increase as you maintain your personal relationship with God even in the darkest hours of your existence.
- Your faith and hope will keep you joyful even when you should be depressed. Notice what Solomon said: *A cheerful heart is good medicine, but a crushed spirit dries up the bones.* – Proverbes 17:22.
- Learn to exercise your faith in God even in the darkest hours of your life; it will serve as powerful testimony to God's glory later.

Notes

_____
_____
_____
_____
_____
_____
_____
_____
_____

Chapter 8:

Avoiding Spiritual Plane Crashes

People experience a spiritual plane crash when their spiritual life seems to hit a bottomless pit. In this case, spiritual burnout is the result, causing many to lose their spiritual fervor. Families or individuals who go through a painful divorce, the loss of a loved one, or a prolonged crisis tend to experience what I call a spiritual plane crash. There are times some believers may even fall into chronic depression, believing that their situations are hopeless. From a human stand point, it is difficult to emerge from such a crash. However, for some reason, God likes to use these situations to allow His glory to shine through us.

There are at least four misconceptions that can lead believers to experience a spiritual plane crash:

- "My situation is hopeless."
- "I will never survive this."
- "I'm the only one on Earth in this crisis."
- "Death is better than living through this painful situation."

Let us read Elijah's experience: *Now Ahab told Jezebel everything Elijah had done and how he had killed all the prophets with the sword. So Jezebel sent a messenger to Elijah to say, "May the gods deal with me, be it ever so severely, if by this time tomorrow I do not make your life like that of one of them."*

Elijah was afraid[a] and ran for his life. When he came to

Beersheba in Judah, he left his servant there, while he himself went a day's journey into the wilderness. He came to a broom bush, sat down under it and prayed that he might die. "I have had enough, LORD," he said. "Take my life; I am no better than my ancestors." Then he lay down under the bush and fell asleep.

All at once an angel touched him and said, "Get up and eat."6 He looked around, and there by his head was some bread baked over hot coals, and a jar of water. He ate and drank and then lay down again.

The angel of the LORD came back a second time and touched him and said, "Get up and eat, for the journey is too much for you." So he got up and ate and drank. Strengthened by that food, he traveled forty days and forty nights until he reached Horeb, the mountain of God. There he went into a cave and spent the night. And the word of the LORD came to him: "What are you doing here, Elijah?"

He replied, "I have been very zealous for the LORD God Almighty. The Israelites have rejected your covenant, torn down your altars, and put your prophets to death with the sword. I am the only one left, and now they are trying to kill me too.

The LORD said, "Go out and stand on the mountain in the presence of the LORD, for the LORD is about to pass by. - 1 Kings 19:1–11.

Notice the downward path followed by Elijah in his moment of depression:

- He felt that his situation was hopeless.
- He went into hiding because he thought he could not survive the crisis.
- He thought he was the only one left to be killed.
- He asked God to take his life.

That's exactly what happens when any believer experiences a spiritual plane crash, or when our spirituality hits the bottomless pit. In order to illustrate some key points, let us consider some common causes of plane crashes.

- *Pilot errors.* Up to 50 percent of air plane crashes are due to pilot errors. Either a pilot makes a mistake while operating the controls or makes a poor decision about flying in adverse conditions. Most poor decisions are made during a crisis in our life than other stable moments. I purposefully chose not to make any major decisions in any adverse conditions. Making decisions while you are discouraged, fearful, angry, depressed, or experiencing any emotional imbalance will cause you to experience a spiritual crash. I call these poor decisions pilot errors, because you are the pilot of your destiny. The decisions you make will inevitably affect your destiny constructively or negatively.

- *Mechanical errors.* They can prevent the plane from flying, landing safely, or taking off correctly. When we fail to maintain our spiritual life through prayer, Bible study, and meditation, it's easy to experience a spiritual plane crash. This may hinder your progress in all the vital areas of your life.

- *Air traffic control errors.* They could lead to a collision between two planes or a mistaken taken off or landing. It's easy to be confused in times of hardships if we don't take time to seek the guidance of the Holy Spirit. The Holy Spirit should be our immediate inspiration and guidance. That's why you should pray daily for the power of the Holy Spirit to overtake your life. He will cause your plane to fly safely even in turbulent weathers.

- *Maintenance negligence.* When an aircraft is not properly maintained according to FAA regulations, it may cause a plane crash. Just as maintenance negligence can cause a crash, we can crash spiritually if we fail to prioritize our spiritual life. It should be the fuel for all other activities. This most important aspect of a believer's life often takes a back seat. Whenever that happens, a spiritual crash may follow. When we focus more on our spiritually, we are better equipped to cope with life's challenges.

- ***Adverse weather conditions.*** Ice, snow, fog, and winds can all affect how a plane performs in the air. Ice on the wings or strong gusts wind could lead to a crash, especially in the case of inexperienced pilots. When experiencing major problems, Christians should always be careful not to compromise their faith. This may lead to a spiritual plane crash. Christians who use their problems as an opportunity to rise higher in their relationship to the Lord will be strengthened and become more mature as they go through life. Problems can be a bridge to so many blessings in our life that we would not experience had we not faced those problems.

- ***Fueling errors.*** Running out of fuel during a flight can cause crash landings. The principles of the word of God should be the primary fuel for a stable Christian life. When we fail to fuel our thoughts with these principles, we should expect to run out of spiritual fuel. This is a spiritual disaster that we should avoid, because planes do not fly without fuel.

- ***Bird strikes.*** Birds striking have accounted to two hundred deaths worldwide in the last twenty years, according to FAA. Bird strikes are identical to major unexpected trials that may cause immature Christians to lose hope and falter in their relationship with the Lord. As a believer, you need to prepare spiritually, mentally, and physically for any unexpected challenge. You never know when a major crisis will hit. The best way to avoid crashes from an unexpected bird strike is to strengthen your spiritual walk with God, knowing you have nothing to fear, because He is with you.

The main purpose of the enemy's repeated persecution is to cause us to experience spiritual plane crashes. He knows for sure that every time you doubt, it causes you to look down. And the more you look down, the more he will damage your belief system until it's almost impossible for you to look up. However, upward-focused prayers will do just the opposite. They will cause you to look up to the Lord, by faith, in order for the impossible to become more than possible. They will cause you to realize that our God specializes in things that are impossible. They will also cause you to banish doubt from your life, since doubt can prevent you from experiencing the fullness of God's manifestation. The devil knows that your deliverance will come from above, not below. That's why it troubles him every time you look up to God in prayer. Here's what the psalmist said:

> Focusing upward implies that our faith is in God, not in men.

> *I lift up my eyes to the mountains—*
>
> *where does my help come from?*
>
> *My help comes from the LORD,*
>
> *the Maker of heaven and earth.*
>
> *He will not let your foot slip—*
>
> *he who watches over you will not slumber;*
>
> *indeed, he who watches over Israel*
>
> *will neither slumber nor sleep.*
>
> *The LORD watches over you—*
>
> *the LORD is your shade at your right hand;*
>
> *the sun will not harm you by day,*
>
> *nor the moon by night.*
>
> *The LORD will keep you from all harm—*
>
> *he will watch over your life;*
>
> *the LORD will watch over your coming and going*
>
> *both now and forevermore." – Psalm 121:1–8.*

The psalmist's admonishment to look up to the hills is a vital indication that he was familiar with the hills and he was enchanted by them. He understood that the answer to his petitions would not come from the hills. The message he wanted to convey is, as you look up to the hills, know that your help will not come from them, but from the Lord. *Where does my help come from? My help comes from the Lord, the maker of heaven and earth.* – Psalm 121:2. We now understand that the upward look is not really directed to the hills, but to the Lord who is the maker of heaven and earth. He alone is able to answer our prayers as we exercise our faith in Him.

Your spiritual plane will not crash if you focus upward. Focusing upward implies that our faith is in God, not in men. That's why we don't look down to men for our help and answers; we look upward to our Lord. Jesus, in His earthly ministry, was accustomed to looking up to heaven in order to direct His supplication to His father in heaven. Here's what He did even before this miracle took place: *Taking the five loaves and the two fish and looking up to heaven, he gave thanks and broke the loaves. Then he gave them to his disciples to distribute to the people. He also divided the two fish among them all. They all ate and were satisfied, and the disciples picked up twelve basketfuls of broken pieces of bread and fish. The number of the men who had eaten was five thousand.* – Marc 6:41–44.

Notice that the first thing that He did while performing this great miracle was to look up to heaven. This is what I rightly call upward-focused prayer. This clearly should inspire all of us to look up to God for our answers. For some it seems easier to trust men than to trust God. This is looking downward, where they will never find the answers they are looking for. No wonder they tend to get discouraged. When we look down we can only get discouraged; when we look up we can only get encouraged. It's as simple as that. As we make a conscious effort to look up, we tend to acquire the motivation to pray and trust God for our miracles in due season. It even inspires consistency in our prayer life. The psalmist said: *My voice shall you hear in the morning, O Lord; in the morning will I direct my prayer unto thee, and will look up"; unto thee lift I up mine eyes, O thou that dwells in the heavens. Behold, as the eyes of servants look unto the hands of their master, and as the eyes of a maiden unto the hand of her mistress; so our eyes wait upon the Lord our God, until he have mercy upon us* – Psalm 5:3; 123:1,2. This implies a childlike dependence upon God for the answer to our prayer in times of needs.

> Only God is able to supply all your needs.

Practice upward-focused prayers because they can move mountains. They help us to expand our faith to look up to God with great expectancy without doubting. They help us to view God as a loving and compassionate father who takes pleasure in picking up his child. Notice what we read in Psalm 103: *Like as a father pitieth his children so the Lord pitieth them that fear Him.*

Points worth special attention

- Inspect your spiritual plane regularly to avoid mechanical errors.
- Control your traffic; know who you are, where you are, and where you want to go. If you don't, it may create collision and confusion which could be fatal to your destiny.
- Conduct regular maintenance on your plane for efficiency as you continue to focus on your goals.
- Make sure you have enough fuel to fly. Get enough physical, mental, and spiritual fuel for your life journey with God.
- Beware of spiritual bird strikes. Bird strikes are those dream-killers who get their satisfaction from crashing your plane. Identify them early enough to distance yourself from them.
- *Look up to God daily for answers to your upward-focused prayers. Look unto me, and be ye saved, all the ends of the earth; for I am God, and there is none else* – Isaiah 45:22.
- Look up to God daily for answers to your difficulties, vexations, trials, temptations, uncertainties, distress, pain, and fears. He will lift you up.
- Instead of looking down for answers, look up to God. We like

to depend on friends for help that we can't depend on. It's time to depend on God. *And my God will meet all your needs according to the riches of his glory in Christ Jesus.* – Philippians 4:19. Only God is able to supply all your needs.

- The blessings of the storehouse of the Lord can satisfy every human need. If we lack them, it is because we fail to look up. I can assure that your spiritual plane will not crash if you intentionally look up to God in adverse situations.

Notes

_____
_____
_____
_____
_____
_____
_____
_____
_____
_____
_____
_____

Notes

Chapter 9:

The Power of Your Mind to Renew Itself

The caterpillar's concept - If you are seeking to experience personal transformation through a mountain top spiritual experience with God, I encourage you to carefully consider the caterpillar's concept. It's amazing how a caterpillar can experience a miraculous metamorphosis that allows it to be transformed into a butterfly. That marvelous revelation from nature should teach us the importance of a remarkable spiritual transformation in a believer's life.

I like how nature reveals the process of transformation that a caterpillar goes through before becoming a butterfly. It's an interesting thing to watch how God uses nature to teach us one of the most vital and meaningful lessons in life.

Children may find the grade school explanation of how a caterpillar becomes a butterfly to be boring. Perhaps it is the reason why so many grade school children pay little attention to science. Besides, a lot of important details are skipped when the story is told. Here's how the story usually goes: Caterpillar crawls to find a perfect spot, then it covers itself in a cocoon. After enough time has passed a butterfly will emerge from it. No, caterpillars do not simply hide inside their chrysalis and after a few days emerge with wings. What happens inside is that the caterpillar releases an enzyme that digests every tissue of the caterpillar. If you'll imagine it, it would be like melting an ice.

Inside the caterpillar there are the "imaginal disks" which act as the transforming agents when the metamorphosis starts. These "imaginal disks" transform into the wings, legs, organs, and antennae of the butterfly.

During the first four days the inside of the chrysalis is the remnants of the dissolved caterpillar, literally a liquid. This is when the magic happens. The cells inside the chrysalis start growing and arranging themselves to form new tissues, innards of the caterpillar, digestive system, the heart, nervous system, and literally everything. So, the caterpillar went from a caterpillar to liquid form to butterfly. Let us consider four principles from a caterpillar's metamorphosis that should serve as spiritual lessons for anyone seeking spiritual transformation through prayer.

> "Be still and know that I am God."

Principle one: Caterpillar crawls to find a perfect spot; then, it covers itself in a cocoon. After enough time has passed, a butterfly will emerge from it. This first stage of the caterpillar's metamorphosis teaches us about the necessity to create time for prayer, meditation, and even fasting in the quietness of our prayer closet. Notice what God said: "Be still and know that I am God." This is clearly an invitation to experience spiritual transformation through meditation, prayer, and fasting. As you do so, you will inevitably witness positive changes in your life.

Principle two: The caterpillar has to eliminate every old tissue in order to experience a brand new transformation. It releases an enzyme that digests every tissue. Without this process there would not be any transformation. In order for you to experience the blessings of spiritual transformation, you have to get rid of all old habits and replace them with new ones that will assist you in your progress. The willingness to have a fresh start with a new mentality is what will pave the way for miracles in your life. Obviously you're reading this book because you desire positive changes in your journey with God. However, in order for those changes to take place, you have to let go of anything that may hold you back.

Principle three: The caterpillar has "transforming agents." Inside the caterpillar, there are the "imaginal disks" which act as these agents when the metamorphosis starts. These "imaginal disks" transform into the wings, legs, organs, and antennae of the butterfly. We may compare the agents in the caterpillar with God's transforming power. The power of the Holy Spirit is capable of allowing us to experience a miraculous transformation in our relationship with God.

Principle four: The caterpillar has to dissolve completely into a liquid in order to experience metamorphosis. The caterpillar metamorphosis goes from a caterpillar, to liquid form, and finally to a beautiful and colorful butterfly with the amazing power to fly. Positive changes take place in a believer's life when they are born again through Christ. You become a new person with a new focus, new desires, new dreams, and a new mentality.

The caterpillar's patience and perseverance in the transformation process is remarkable and amazing. It goes from the slavery of crawling to the freedom to fly and never returns to a crawling caterpillar again. That's what I call transformation.

In Luke's gospel we read the following statement about the transformation of our Savior on the mount of transfiguration: *And as He prayed, the fashion of his countenance was altered, and His raiment was white and glistering."* – Luke 9:29. This is very much comparable, in a certain sense, to the caterpillar's experience described above. As Jesus took time to pray and connect with heaven, He was able to experience a transforming power which couldn't escape the attention of those present – Peter, James, and John:

About eight days after Jesus said this, he took Peter, James, and John with him and went up onto a mountain to pray. 29 As

he was praying, the appearance of his face changed, and his clothes became as bright as a flash of lightning. 30 Two men, Moses and Elijah, appeared in glorious splendor, talking with Jesus. 31 They spoke about his departure,[a] which he was about to bring to fulfillment at Jerusalem. 32 Peter and his companions were very sleepy, but when they became fully awake, they saw his glory and the two men standing with him. 33 As the men were leaving Jesus, Peter said to him, "Master, it is good for us to be here. Let us put up three shelters—one for you, one for Moses and one for Elijah."
– Luke 9:29–33.

Peter, James, and John as well as angels were the witnesses to this sublime and unearthly scene. One of the primary purposes of this scene is to reveal the power of prayer and faith. As we read it, we see clearly that prayer indeed changes things. When, by faith, you connect to God for certain things to change in your life, be assured that they will change. God reacts to our faith and intense prayer. Notice that the transfiguration took place as Jesus was praying,

And as He prayed, the fashion of His countenance was altered, and His raiment was white and glistering.

Before He prayed He was a man of sorrow acquainted with grief, but prayer brought transformation in His life. Prayer changes things. Prayer generates genuine transformation.

People with the caterpillar's mentality who truly want changes will experience them through persistence in prayer. As we focus on some instances in the Bible, where prayer was the means for the miracle of change and transformation, let us read and reflect on the faith building exercises that pave the way for the following miracles.

Bible reading exercise

Read carefully each of the following miracles from the word of God. Try to go over the details as many times as possible. After reading them, highlight all the steps that precede the miracles. Pray and ask God to provide you with those spiritual tools in your own prayer life.

Our Lord's own experience: *"Then Jesus came from Galilee to the Jordan to be baptized by John. But John tried to deter him, saying, "I need to be baptized by you, and do you come to me?"*

Jesus replied, "Let it be so now; it is proper for us to do this to fulfill all righteousness." Then John consented.

As soon as Jesus was baptized, he went up out of the water. At that moment heaven was opened, and he saw the Spirit of God descending like a dove and alighting on him. And a voice from heaven said, "This is my Son, whom I love; with him I am well pleased." – Matthew 3:13–17.

Steps that led to the miracle

- Jesus insisted on doing what's right and so should you.
- God the Father honored his conviction by confirming his action. Your actions must be in line with the will of God in order for God to confirm them.

In the following biblical story, we will study the transforming power of persistence through faith, perseverance, and patience, which motivated Jesus to heal the demon-possessed daughter of a Canaanite woman.

Leaving that place, Jesus withdrew to the region of Tyre and Sidon. A Canaanite woman from that vicinity came to him, crying out, "Lord, Son of David, have mercy on me! My daughter is demon-possessed and suffering terribly." Jesus did not answer a word. So his disciples came to him and urged him, "Send her away, for she keeps crying out after us."

He answered, "I was sent only to the lost sheep of Israel."

The woman came and knelt before him. "Lord, help me!" she said.

He replied, "It is not right to take the children's bread and toss it to the dogs."

"Yes it is, Lord," she said. "Even the dogs eat the crumbs that fall from their master's table."

Then Jesus said to her, "Woman, you have great faith! Your request is granted." And her daughter was healed at that moment. – Matthew 15:22–28.

She understood that "Faith is the assurance of things hoped for, and the evidence of things not seen." Faith is not something that you can feel, it is a confidence that you build as you commune with God on a regular basis.

She was not willing to give up until she experienced her miracle. Faith gives the courage to fight until your last breath. That's why after her daughter was delivered, Jesus told her: *Woman, you have great faith.*

As we mentioned previously, faith and tenacity caused the blind bartimaeus to receive his sight:

Then they came to Jericho. As Jesus and his disciples, together with a large crowd, were leaving the city, a blind man, Bartimaeus (which means "son of Timaeus"), was sitting by the roadside begging. When he heard that it was Jesus of Nazareth, he began to shout, "Jesus, Son of David, have mercy on me!"

Many rebuked him and told him to be quiet, but he shouted all the more, "Son of David, have mercy on me!" Jesus stopped and said, "Call him."

So they called to the blind man, "Cheer up! On your feet! He's calling you." Throwing his cloak aside, he jumped to his feet and came to Jesus.

"What do you want me to do for you?" Jesus asked him.

The blind man said, "Rabbi, I want to see."

"Go," said Jesus, "your faith has healed you." Immediately he received his sight and followed Jesus along the road. – Mark 10:46–52.

The blind man's road map to transformation

He cried louder in spite of those trying to calm him down. Obstacles should motivate you to pray harder instead of allowing your prayers to take a back seat.

The Lord heard his voice from the beginning, but He wanted him to persevere. The same people who were trying to discourage him, came back and told him: "Be of good cheer." The persistence of the blind man should motivate us to fight even in the face of contrary evidence.

By faith Peter caught the exact fish that had enough money in its belly to pay his tax and that of his Lord.

After Jesus and His disciples arrived in Capernaum, the

collectors of the two-drachma temple tax came to Peter and asked, "Doesn't your teacher pay the temple tax?"

"Yes, he does," he replied.

When Peter came into the house, Jesus was the first to speak. "What do you think, Simon?" he asked. "From whom do the kings of the earth collect duty and taxes—from their own children or from others?"

"From others," Peter answered.

"Then the children are exempt," Jesus said to him. "But so that we may not cause offense, go to the lake and throw out your line. Take the first fish you catch; open its mouth and you will find a four-drachma coin. Take it and give it to them for my tax and yours." – Matthew 17:24–27.

Peter's road map to his miracle: Peter could have questioned the Lord's command, but chose to obey His Lord by faith. Faith gave Peter the strength to obey God's command. Peter learned that God performs financial miracles for those who trust Him and follow His command.

By Faith, Moses' mother transformed the life of her son

Now a man of the tribe of Levi married a Levite woman, and she became pregnant and gave birth to a son. When she saw that he was a fine child, she hid him for three months. But when she could hide him no longer, she got a papyrus basket[a] for him and coated it with tar and pitch. Then she placed the child in it and put it among the reeds along the bank of the Nile. His sister stood at a distance to see what would happen to him.

Then Pharaoh's daughter went down to the Nile to bathe, and her attendants were walking along the riverbank. She saw the basket among the reeds and sent her female slave to get it. She opened it and saw the baby. He was crying, and she felt sorry for him. "This is one of the Hebrew babies," she said.

Then his sister asked Pharaoh's daughter, "Shall I go and get one of the Hebrew women to nurse the baby for you?"

"Yes, go," she answered. So the girl went and got the baby's mother. Pharaoh's daughter said to her, "Take this baby and nurse him for me, and I will pay you." So the woman took the baby and nursed him. When the child grew older, she took him to Pharaoh's daughter and he became her son. She named him Moses, saying, "I drew him out of the water."

Her roadmap to transforming her son's life: She was willing to take a risk by faith. Prayer caterpillars are not afraid to take a risk for change. Her faith provided her wisdom which gave her confidence to take the right action. As a result, she got paid to raise her own son.

By faith, God transformed the lives of His people. The red sea was divided and Israel passed through it, walking on dry land.

Then Moses stretched out his hand over the sea, and all that night the LORD drove the sea back with a strong east wind and turned it into dry land. The waters were divided, and the Israelites went through the sea on dry ground, with a wall of water on their right and on their left.

The Egyptians pursued them, and all Pharaoh's horses and chariots and horsemen followed them into the sea. During the last watch of the night the LORD looked down from the pillar of fire and cloud at the Egyptian army and threw it into confusion. He jammed[b] the wheels of their chariots so that they had difficulty driving. And the Egyptians said, "Let's get away from the Israelites! The LORD is fighting for them against Egypt."

Then the LORD said to Moses, "Stretch out your hand over the sea so that the waters may flow back over the Egyptians and their chariots and horsemen." Moses stretched out his hand over the sea, and at daybreak the sea went back to its place. The Egyptians were fleeing toward it, and the LORD swept them into the sea. The water flowed back and covered the chariots and horsemen—the entire army of Pharaoh that had followed the Israelites into the sea. Not one of them survived.

But the Israelites went through the sea on dry ground, with a wall of water on their right and on their left. That day the LORD saved Israel from the hands of the Egyptians, and Israel saw the Egyptians lying dead on the shore. And when the Israelites saw the mighty hand of the LORD displayed against the Egyptians, the people feared the LORD and put their trust in him and in Moses his servant. – Exodus 14:21-31.

By faith prison doors were opened to Peter and set him free to preach the gospel.

Peter was kept in prison, but the church was earnestly praying to God for him.

The night before Herod was to bring him to trial, Peter was sleeping between two soldiers, bound with two chains, and sentries stood guard at the entrance. Suddenly an angel of the Lord appeared and a light shone in the cell. He struck Peter on the side and woke him up. "Quick, get up!" he said, and the chains fell off Peter's wrists.

Then the angel said to him, "Put on your clothes and sandals." And Peter did so. "Wrap your cloak around you and follow me," the angel told him. Peter followed him out of the prison, but he had no idea that what the angel was doing was really happening; he thought he was seeing a vision. They passed the first and second guards and came to the iron gate leading to the city. It opened for them by itself, and they went through it. When they had walked the length of one street, suddenly the angel left him.

Then Peter came to himself and said, "Now I know without a doubt that the Lord has sent his angel and rescued me from Herod's clutches and from everything the Jewish people were hoping would happen."

When this had dawned on him, he went to the house of Mary the mother of John, also called Mark, where many people had gathered and were praying. Peter knocked at the outer entrance, and a servant named Rhoda came to answer the door. When she recognized Peter's voice, she was so overjoyed she ran back without opening it and exclaimed, "Peter is at the door!"

"You're out of your mind," they told her. When she kept insisting that it was so, they said, "It must be his angel."

But Peter kept on knocking, and when they opened the door and saw him, they were astonished. Peter motioned with his hand for them to be quiet and described how the Lord had brought him out of prison. "Tell James and the other brothers and sisters about *this," he said, and then he left for another place. – Acts 12:5–17.*

A short prayer of faith saved Peter from drowning

Then Peter got down out of the boat, walked on the water and came toward Jesus. But when he saw the wind, he was afraid and, beginning to sink, cried out, "Lord, save me!"

Immediately Jesus reached out his hand and caught him. "You of little faith," he said, "why did you doubt?"

And when they climbed into the boat, the wind died down. Then those who were in the boat worshiped him, saying, "Truly you are the Son of God." – Matthew 14:30, 31.

Peter lost his balance and began to drown after taking his eyes off Jesus. He began to feel afraid because he lost his focus. The sincerity of his cry to Jesus, and his willingness to be rescued earned him the miracle that saved his life.

It's not the length of the prayer that matters, but your faith. As you pray God will sometimes make you walk on the high waters of life. But, you should never take your eyes off of Him.

Mark's version of the story of the woman with the issue of blood

And a woman was there who had been subject to bleeding for twelve years. She had suffered a great deal under the care of many doctors and had spent all she had, yet instead of getting better she grew worse. When she heard about Jesus, she came up behind him in the crowd and touched his cloak, because she thought, "If I just touch his clothes, I will be healed." Immediately her bleeding stopped and she felt in her body that she was freed from her suffering.

At once Jesus realized that power had gone out from him. He turned around in the crowd and asked, "Who touched my clothes?"

"You see the people crowding against you," his disciples answered, "and yet you can ask, 'Who touched me?' "

But Jesus kept looking around to see who had done it. Then the woman, knowing what had happened to her, came and fell at his feet and, trembling with fear, told him the whole truth. He said to her, "Daughter, your faith has healed YOU." – Marc 5: 25-34

The childlike faith behind her transformation

The faith behind her touch has earned her this great miracle, "If I just touch his clothes, I will be healed." I call this a caterpillar prayer. She strongly believes by touching his clothes, transformation would take place.

Notice what Jesus said to her: "Daughter, your faith has healed you." Faith will bring transformation in your life that will cause you to fly like a caterpillar.

As you went through the Bible reading exercises above, you realized the importance of faith and action in your quest to experience the power of God in order to experience spiritual transformation. These faith stories from the Bible should build your faith and cause you to trust God for any positive changes you aspire to. As you develop the patience and perseverance of the caterpillar, you will discover that, with faith in God, the sky is the limit.

Points worth special attention

- In order to experience spiritual transformation you have to create time for prayer, fasting, and meditation.
- Getting rid of old habits that hinder your progress will cause you to experience positive changes.
- Spiritual transformation will pave the way for God to intervene miraculously in every area of needs in your life.
- Seek to develop the patience of the caterpillar with the assurance that change will come inevitably.
- Seek to develop the perseverance of the caterpillar. This will allow you to maintain your motivation until you reach your goals in due season.

- Boldness, willingness, motivation, and action are not just words. They are life changing principles.
- Keep your attention strongly focused on your goals in order not to be distracted by the daily events of your life.
- Never underestimate the power of faith and tenacity. They work hand-in-hand.

Notes

Chapter 10:

The Power to 'Peck' into Destiny

Ask and it will be given to you; seek and you will find; knock and the door will be opened to you. For everyone who asks receives; the one who seeks finds; and to the one who knocks, the door will be opened.

The woodpecker's concept. The greatest accomplishments in the world, past, present, and future may be summarized in three verbs: ask, seek and knock. The woodpecker's concept focuses on the limitless reward of perseverance through asking, seeking, and knocking.

Those three verbs describe in concrete terms the essential qualities of woodpeckers as they carry on their daily activities. The following explanation of their task will help us understand why we must peck hard every day into our destiny.

Perseverance. Their perseverance is demonstrated in their ability to drill holes in trees for later use. They never seem to get tired of pecking. They continue to peck until they reach their ideal goal. This is a vital and meaningful lesson that we may learn from woodpeckers. When we have a goal in mind, we should peck until we reach it.

Environment Cleaner. Woodpeckers are excellent insects destroyers. By destroying the insects, they create a cleaner and safer environment that makes it possible for them to continue on with their tasks. People tend to be distracted and discouraged by annoying nuisances in the way of their progress as they try to ask, seek, and knock with the purpose of reaching their goals. However, we should identify our annoying nuisances and eliminate them from our physical and spiritual environment in order for us to move on smoothly with our activities. Unless you eliminate them for a cleaner personal environment, they will continue to bug you.

Good eyesight, hearing, and smell. Woodpeckers have excellent eyesight as well as keen hearing and sensitive smell. These qualities would help you to be more focused on your goal by detecting your obstacles early enough to prepare for them. This opens the door for efficient work accomplishments.

Adaptability and tenacity. Woodpeckers are known for their adaptability and tenacity. When they find the right environment and work area, they make sure that they adapt to every detail so that nothing will catch them by surprise in their persistent pecking. They do not give up until the task is fulfilled. With this kind of mentality, success in any good cause is guaranteed.

Goals and ideals oriented. Woodpeckers are goal-and-ideals oriented. Like woodpeckers, you should establish your goals and ideals first. Know what you want to accomplish and peck hard into it until the task is fully completed.

Punctuality and vigilance. Woodpeckers start working early in the morning and are always on schedule. This should teach us the importance of punctuality and vigilance through persistence, dedication, and determination. This is nature's way of providing us with lessons that will equip us for success and achievements which will yield great rewards. It's letting us know that with punctuality and vigilance through persistence, dedication, and determination we can make it. We must remain vigilant, while discovering a routine that will get us closer and closer to our destiny. That's the price of hard work.

Woodpeckers teach us how to connect with the earth and how to ground ourselves in nature. They show us rhythm, fertility, Earth's heartbeat, increase of mental/physical activities, and the beat of life. They aid in our ability to find deeper meanings and hidden qualities of patterns and coincidences. Are you drumming and creating your own beat? They teach us that you can do that safely by awakening new mental faculties. Woodpeckers teach us to balance the spiritual and mental aspects with the physical world for harmony. Woodpeckers are great examples of tenacity, patience and straightforward actions in our daily activities.

Woodpeckers understand that faith without work is dead, and

work without a purpose is null.

When you become really active in putting your faith to work, you will not be afraid to ask, seek, and knock, because you will automatically be driven by your purpose. Without that purpose, everything you do will be meaningless. Your purpose and determination will keep you motivated on a daily basis. It will be as simple as turning on the key in the ignition of your car. Once the engine is running, it's easier to set your transmission on drive and keep moving. At this level you can drive as fast and as far as you want if the car is well equipped with everything necessary for a smooth ride. When you don't match your faith with your purpose, it's like having a brand new car, but for some reason, you just let it sit there without having a good reason to drive it. In this case you would not be able to reap the benefits of the car even though it already belongs to you.

The Bible defines faith as, *The assurance of things hoped for, and the evidence of things not seen.* It's already yours but you have to purposefully act on it. So, it's time to get to work!

Realizing how much a single woodpecker is able to accomplish just by pecking into the wood reminds us that it's impossible to succeed without purposeful works.

Notice what James said: *Faith by itself, if it does not have works, is dead. But someone will say, "You have faith, and I have works." Show me your faith without your works, and I will show you my faith by my works.* – James 2:17–18.

This gives us a glimpse of God's attitude toward faith and action. He wants us to match our faith with our action even when it appears challenging to do so. Action is what's going to get the job done as we move on. In this particular scripture quoted above, James clearly opens our eyes to the fact that believing and praying should not be sufficient in our quest for the power to fly. We'll begin to see positive changes only and only when we deliberately choose to be very active in the process of pursuing our destiny.

Let us analyze briefly the three action verbs that Jesus used in order to teach us the importance of connecting our action to our faith. You and I both know that asking is synonymous to making contacts. You have to make contacts in order to ask, and by asking, *it shall be given unto you.*

Contacts allow you to pave the way for God to bless your endeavor. In today's world they use the word networking. Here's what it means: *Networking is the practice of making contact and exchanging information with other people, groups or institutions. Usually, networking occurs with other people who have interests in similar areas. The goal of the networking relationship may be to further your personal employment opportunities or to cultivate new clients or the expansion of business relationships. Networking is also a term of art used in the computer industry.*

Whatever your goals may be; whatever your plan is, you need to network. It simply means contacting the right people. After having prayed for wisdom and guidance on a regular basis, your next step should be to network with the right people that will help you expand in the area of your gift and calling, whether it be ministry, business, politics, or any other field you strongly believe God empowered you to explore in life. As you ask, make contacts, or network, you will surely discover that there are others who support your goals and desire to connect with you to reach them. As you begin to network, be assured that God has already gathered the people with whom you will network. They are out there waiting for you to ask. So, don't be afraid to ask. That's why Jesus said: *Ask and it shall be given unto you.* It's as simple as that.

It means:

- To require. – Genesis 34:12
- To seek counsel. – Isaiah 30:2
- To expect. – Luke 12:9
- To be in need of something. – Revelation 3:14–17

God made asking the medium of all blessings because it implies that someone at the other end will be willing and able to supply what you need to pursue your destiny. Asking also demonstrates, in the right context, the reasonableness of faith and action.

Again, I want to emphasize the importance of networking for those of you who are in ministry or business. It is the single most powerful tool available for you to share your plans and rally the support you need in order to move forward.

Networking is about making connections and building enduring, mutually beneficial relationships. Why not start today by asking God to inspire you in ensuring you meet the "right" people to include in your network and expand your sphere of influence. *Ultimately, it's not about who you know ... but who knows you!*

Ask any pastor, senior executive, politician, community leader or successful salesperson which single skill or habit helped them excel in their career. An overwhelming majority will respond with one simple word: Networking. Once, you have been empowered by God to fulfill your mission, He will pave the way for you to meet the right people.

Networking is extremely important, and should comprise a major fraction of your plan of action.

We are constantly bombarded with advertisements, emails, status updates, special offers, and sales pitches creating a cluttered message. However, personal relationships should be the primary tool that will enable you and your organization to stand out, rise above the noise and remain top of mind.

Relationships are the catalyst for success. By that I mean vertical relationships. Work daily toward strengthening your relationship with God and those He allows you to network with. People do business with those they like and trust.

> The one who seeks will find

Serve as a resource, help others succeed; and as you do so, your circle will become stronger and more trustworthy.

Networking provides the most productive, most proficient and most enduring tactic to build relationships. To succeed you must continually connect with new people, cultivate emerging relationships and leverage your network.

Now that you have read about the powerful connotation of the verb 'ask,' it's time to consider the second verb: 'seek.'

Seeking implies special interest on our part, by emphasizing whatever is essential. It implies that special treasures of the kingdom are waiting for you in God's storehouse if you put your faith and action to work. Matthew 11:25; 13:11.

Seeking also implies that the blessings of the Kingdom of God, if sought earnestly, can be accessed. That's why Jesus said, *the one who seeks will find.* We also consider why knocking is used.

Knocking suggests perseverance in spite of major obstacles. The doors are closed right before our eyes, but we knock anyway with a strong conviction that they will open up. You might have read the story of Jacob's persistence at Jabbok. Genesis 32:26

Knocking suggests motivation and commitment. When we are motivated and committed we persistently continue to knock even when we don't see any signs that the doors will be opened. We just know without the shadow of a doubt that they will be opened. That's the woodpecker's approach.

Believers who are not intimated by obstacles and challenges in their mission always get more than what they sought. That's why the Bible says: *Now unto Him that is able to do exceeding abundantly above all that we ask or think, according to the power that worketh in us.* – Ephesians 3:20.

I strongly believe that if we allow our action to match our faith, we would enjoy the blessings of God in so many miraculous ways that we would not have enough room to contain them. If we trust God for our miracles and act upon them even before they happen, God would open doors in our lives that we would never imagine. Notice what James said:

> *Ask and ye shall receive.*
>
> *Seek and ye shall find.*
>
> *Knock and it shall be opened unto you.* – James 4:1–3.

These are God's promises to you if you persevere in faith and action. These are God's promises to you if you peck through your destiny like woodpeckers.

Points worth special attention

- The woodpecker's tenacity should inspire you to continue to peck until you reach your destiny.
- I encourage you to develop the winner's mentality. Winners never quit; quitters never win.
- If you ask, seek, and knock, God will allow you to reap more than you ever expect.
- Don't be afraid of obstacles and challenges; they will pave the way for greater success.
- Even when the doors are shut tight, keep knocking anyway; they cannot resist your persistence.
- Practice the punctuality and vigilance of woodpeckers. This world needs people with that kind of commitment. It will be very rewarding.

Chapter 11:

Changing from a Sundown Mentality to a Sunrise Mentality

God created us with the ability to shine, adapt, and adjust in all circumstances and conditions in this life. That's why, with the right mentality and attitude, we can still shine in spite of our challenges. You probably notice when it's time for the sun to shine, there is absolutely nothing that can prevent it from shining. You should also notice that the sun shines with the purpose of benefiting anything it influences. With this in mind, let us consider the primary benefits of the sun.

- The Sun is the brightest and most familiar object in the sky. Life on Earth would not be possible without it.
- The food we eat exists because of sunlight falling on green plants, and the fuel we burn comes either from such plants, or was accumulated by them (in the forms of coal, oil and natural gas) long ago.
- Without the sun the Earth would not be fit for life. Life, as we know it, needs liquid water, and Earth is the only planet to have it: without the sun, Earth would be an icy rock in space. Even now, Earth is probably the only place in our solar system fit for life.
- We need the sun. Without it, there wouldn't be any life on Earth; we'd just have a cold ball of rock floating through space.

- The sun keeps us in place. Even though the Earth is about 93 million miles from the sun, the sun's gravity can reach out and hang onto us. Without this pull of gravity, we'd just fly off into space, away from the warmth and light of the sun, and out into the cold black of space. This is a very important job that the sun does for us, and makes everything else possible.
- The sun helps with the tides. Most of the daily ocean tides happen because of the moon. But we experience our highest and lowest tides when the sun, Earth and moon are lined up in a row.
- The sun keeps us warm. Every spot on Earth is receiving an average of 342 watts of energy from the sun. This is an average across every part of the Earth, and includes both night and day. This number is much higher for locations near the equator. Most of this energy bounces off the Earth and goes back into space, but our atmosphere acts like a blanket, trapping some of this heat from the sun. Thanks to the sun, we enjoy a nice average temperature worldwide.

People with a sunrise mentality live a purposeful life. Because they live with a purpose, their focus is up, not down. They tend to be more interested in the rising of the sun. They focus more on the positive instead of the negative side of life. They see hope in just about any situation. This category believes that after every sunset there is a sunrise. They strongly believe that, not only they have a purpose for being here on earth, but they can influence people positively and constructively.

On the other hand, people with a sunset mentality tend to focus more on the setting of the sun than its rising. In other words, they are more pessimistic than optimistic. They spend their energy worrying about the dark side of life instead of smelling the roses. They tend to believe that they are not capable of influencing anyone positively.

What we should realize is that the Earth really needs the sun just as the sun needs the Earth to fulfill its purpose. God created it for a purpose. In the same way, God also created you for a purpose; and you will not be able to fully shine, in anything you do on earth unless you clearly understand your purpose.

A purpose implies a result, end, mean, aim, or goal of an action intentionally undertaken, or of an object being brought into use or existence. That's why, by knowing your purpose for being here on Earth will create in you the desire to shine through everything you accomplish in life.

How do you discover your real purpose in life? First,

you should understand that your purpose is more than some activities like school, work, intention, or plans. Your purpose is much more than that. Your purpose is so gigantic, that it is bigger than you are. Your purpose is the core meaning or reason for being here on Earth. It's that important! This explains why a life without a purpose is meaningless. Your life really begins only after you discover your purpose.

When you face some difficulties in life, you might be tempted to believe that your existence here on Earth is just a mere coincidence. However, it's not so in God's plan for your life. He has already mapped out everything for you. That's why it is important for you to discover your purpose in order to have access to what He has already established for you.

Not knowing your purpose will delay or even cancel God's flow of blessings in your life. Only a purpose driven life will be able to reap God's blessings in due season. It allows you to empty yourself of all life's misconceptions so your creator can fill you up with everything He has purposely designed for you.

I recently read a story about the successful actor Bruce Lee, which I invite you to read as well. It illustrates why you should empty yourself of past misconceptions after discovering your purpose. A martial artist asked Bruce one day to teach him everything he knew about martial arts. Bruce Lee held up two cups, both filled with liquid. "The first cup," he said, "represents all of your knowledge about martial arts. The second cup represents all of my knowledge about martial arts. If you want to fill your cup with my knowledge, you must first empty your cup of your knowledge."

In order for your creator to fulfill His plans for your life, you must be willing to unlearn for the sake of learning. You must make room for the Holy Spirit to occupy your thoughts and actions as you conduct your daily activities. You will wake up every day with a sense of satisfaction knowing you are following His blue print within the confines of your purpose. It's what I call "unlearn in order to learn." You can only do that when you discover your purpose for being here on earth.

Here's how you may discover God's purpose for your life.

- **Be willing to change.** By being willing to change, you will become more open to the process. You will become like the clay in the Potter's hand. Here's what the Bible says: *Yet you, LORD, are our Father. We are the clay, you are the potter; we are all the work of your hand.* – Isaiah 64:8.
- ***Know God's will for your life so that there may not be any conflict between what He wants and what you'd like to***

accomplish. Here's what Paul said: *For who is able to resist his will? But who are you, a human being, to talk back to God? Shall what is formed say to the one who formed it, 'Why did you make me like this?' Does not the potter have the right to make out of the same lump of clay some pottery for special purposes and some for common use?* – Romans 9:19–21.

You must digest well the concept that God is the potter; you're the clay in His hands. As you willingly and totally lean on His wisdom and power, He will mold you and shape your destiny in such a meaningful and powerful way that you will develop a sincere attitude of praise toward Him daily as you continue to peck hard. You will start experiencing major positive changes in your life. As you experience those changes, always remember that just as God created the sun for a purpose, He also created you for a purpose. Millions of people die without ever knowing their purpose. That's why the word of God admonishes us to empty our vessel in order to allow God to equip us and motivate us toward the fulfillment of our purpose. People who reject that possibility will experience major down falls that could have been prevented.

People without a purpose resist changes while developing a sunset mentality that causes them to remain pessimistic and unproductive in many significant areas of their life. Notice what Jeremiah said as he personalized Moab, a small country that refused to change after becoming pessimistic: *Moab hath been at ease from his youth, and he hath settled on his lees, and hath not been emptied from vessel to vessel, neither hath he gone into captivity; therefore his taste remained in him, and his scent hath not changed.* – Jeremiah 48:11.

Moab was a small country with great opportunities and challenges. It was noted mainly for its magnificent vineyards, which were a great natural asset for its progress and development. At that time it was customary to use the ancient process of changing wine from vessel to vessel. Since that process was very familiar, the prophet uses it as a metaphor to illustrate what happens to nations or people who are not opened to changes and progress. Because of Moab's constant refusal to change, Moab was dying of physical as well as spiritual stagnation. Moab fell at ease in spite of its prolonged moral decay. The challenges that Moab faced contributed further to its decay, because when you don't know your purpose, any challenge that could be used as a major highway to your success will become a source of major discouragement. Because believers with the sun's mentality focus on the bright side of life, they know that our checkered experiences have a wonderful power of cleansing effect upon our lives. If taken positively challenges will become opportunities. Here's what Paul said: *We glory in tribulations also; knowing that tribulation worketh patience.* – Romans 5:3.

Now no chastening for the present seemeth to be joyous, but grievous: Nevertheless afterward it yieldeth the peaceable fruit of righteousness unto them which are exercised thereby. – Hebrews 12:11.

The message here is that even tribulations will turn out to be blessings in your life. They grant you access to the major spiritual cleansing and patience you need in order to find and embrace your purpose. King Nebuchadnezzar was amazed to witness how God delivered His people from the tribulations of the Babylonian Kingdom. However, if they had not gone through some tough experiences which convinced them of the power of the true living God, they would not be able to reap those blessings. In spite of hardships they were able to maintain a sunshine mentality. That's what happens when we connect to God. He gives us the power to see and do things His way.

Today, I encourage you to pray earnestly for a sunrise mentality that will help you to focus on the bright side of life. This will serve as a faith-building attitude in your daily endeavors.

Bible Reading Exercise

Read the following Scriptures from the book of Deuteronomy, where God's favor was solicited on Joseph, and see how you can receive that divine favor in your own experience with God. This will lead to the realization that believers with a sunrise mentality are able to look up to God for favor because He causes His sun to rise only on those who trust Him. Joseph is a good biblical example of a blessed man who maintains the right mentality throughout the experiences of his life. After reading the following Scripture, write down in your own words several practical lessons that you have learned from it. You may have to read it several times in order to fully capture its meaning and implication in your own life.

May the LORD bless his land
with the precious dew from heaven above
and with the deep waters that lie below;
with the best the sun brings forth
and the finest the moon can yield;
the with choicest gifts of the ancient mountains
and the fruitfulness of the everlasting hills;
with the best gifts of the earth and its fullness
and the favor of him who dwelt in the burning bush.

> *Let all these rest on the head of Joseph,*
> *on the brow of the prince among[e] his brothers.*
> *In majesty he is like a firstborn bull;*
> *his horns are the horns of a wild ox.*
> *With them he will gore the nations,*
> *even those at the ends of the earth.*
> *Such are the ten thousands of Ephraim.*
> *– Deuteronomy 33:13–17.*

People with a sunshine mentality remain optimistic because they know they have a goodly heritage. Notice what the psalmist had to say:

> *LORD, you alone are my portion and my cup;*
> *you make my lot secure.*
> *The boundary lines have fallen for me in pleasant places;*
> *surely I have a delightful inheritance.*
> *I will praise the LORD, who counsels me;*
> *even at night my heart instructs me.*
> *I keep my eyes always on the LORD.*
> *With him at my right hand, I will not be shaken.*
> *Therefore my heart is glad and my tongue rejoices;*
> *my body also will rest secure,*
> *because you will not abandon me to the realm of the dead,*

> *nor will you let your faithful[b] one see decay.*
> *You make known to me the path of life;*
> *you will fill me with joy in your presence,*
> *with eternal pleasures at your right hand.* – Psalm 16:5-11.

As a true believer, you should rest assured that your love and affections for God are truly worthy of being cherished by Him. That's why you can afford to remain optimistic in any circumstance. That's why He takes pleasure in bestowing His favor on you. He knows you will not allow your blessings to take away your love for Him; instead they will draw you even closer to Him.

Notice how David, by faith, made claim to a wealthy estate because he sees himself as an heir of God's inheritance in spite of major obstacles and difficulties: *Lord, you alone are my portion and my cup; you make my lot secure. The boundary lines have fallen for me in pleasant places.* – Psalm 16:5.

These are the words of someone who sees the bright side of life. Instead of focusing on the setting of the sun, he focuses on its rising. That's when sunlight radiates through every single experience. May that inspire you to always choose a sunrise mentality over a sunset mentality every single day of your spiritual journey.

Points worth special attention

- Chose to live your life with a sunrise mentality by focusing on the bright side of life. Allow God to equip you for handling your challenges.

- Being depressed over your problems will not solve them. Your faith in God will.

- People who are pessimistic tend to be depressed because they have a sunset mentality. Tough times may come unexpectedly. As you deal with them, don't allow them to occupy your thoughts, because whatever occupies your thought will expand.

- In your daily devotion, take a moment to reflect on God's blessings in your life. This will help you maintain an attitude of praise toward the Lord in everything that you do.

- People with a sunrise mentality always seek to influence others positively just as the sun influences the Earth positively in so many ways.

Chapter 12:

The Power to Accept and Receive Life's Inheritance

LORD, you alone are my portion and my cup; you make my lot secure. The boundary lines have fallen for me in pleasant places; surely I have a delightful inheritance. – Psalm 16:5–6.

Psalm 16, for various reasons, is often considered a golden psalm because of the message it conveys. In this psalm David laid claim of a wealthy estate by faith. Contrary to some misconceptions about God's inheritance for his children, He reserves the best for those who trust him and serve him with conviction. What I mean by that is that God blesses you according to your level of faith and personal conviction. Even though His blessings are made available for all who aspire after them, he will not force them on anyone.

There are two important aspects of God's inheritance that separate it from secular inheritance:

God's inheritance implies a wealth of goodness. *And the LORD said, "I will cause all my goodness to pass in front of you, and I will proclaim my name, the LORD, in your presence. I will have mercy on whom I will have mercy, and I will have compassion on whom I will have compassion.* – Exodus 33:19.

Goodness is a special umbrella of blessings that God places above you as you walk with him toward your destiny. This umbrella provides the assurance of His inheritance which you can claim and enjoy. It's on you, but you will not receive until you're fully convinced it's already yours and claim it by faith.

You might be wondering how you may claim something that you hope to have. I wish I could give you a very logical and reasonable answer to that question. But that's not how God operates. He wants you to raise your faith to a higher dimension in order for Him to bless you accordingly. Notice what David said: *You prepare a table before me in the presence of my enemies. You anoint my head with oil; my cup overflows. Surely your goodness and love will follow me all the days of my life.* – Psalm 23:5,6.

Like David, you need to envision yourself as a guest in God's banquet hall. This type of spiritual envisioning will allow you to understand that He is a king, lavishing upon His guests the bounties of His table. And, since God is the host you don't have to fear the plots of the enemies. Just know that His goodness will follow you wherever you are.

God's inheritance implies an abundance of security. Read the following Scriptures while considering this vital aspect of God's inheritance.

There is no one like the God of Jeshurun, who rides across the heavens to help you and on the clouds in His majesty. The eternal God is your refuge, and underneath are the everlasting arms. He will drive out your enemies before you, saying, 'Destroy them!' So Israel will live in safety; Jacob will dwell secure in a land of grain and new wine, where the heavens drop dew. Blessed are you, Israel! Who is like you a people saved by the LORD? He is your shield and helper and your glorious sword. Your enemies will cower before you, and you will tread on their heights.

Verses 26 and 27 deal with God's help which is available to believers of His kingdom and majesty. Every single detail of the universe is under His control. *He rides across the heavens to help you and on the clouds in his majesty. The Eternal God is your refuge and underneath are the everlasting arms.*

As I analyze the word 'security,' I think this portion of the word of God defines it better than any dictionary available on Earth. Divine security means God's help is available for you whenever and wherever you need it. It's already there. This indicates clearly that true security is limitless and can only be accessible through God. My purpose here is not to underestimate the importance of earthly security even though it is very limited. I just want to encourage you to amplify your trust in divine security which is perfect in its nature, and always available any time there is a need for it.

Notice what the next portion of this scriptural passage says: *He will drive out your enemies before you, saying: "Destroy them."*

The word enemy, in this context, stands for anybody or anything standing as a stumbling block in the way of your progress. God promises to handle them for you. The reason why you can depend on His divine security is because it controls both the visible and the invisible, the physical and the spiritual. What some believers don't know is that your invisible or spiritual enemies are greater and stronger than your visible physical enemies. That's why only God can handle them. Without His divine security, there would not be any fence around our lives to protect us against the assaults of our enemies. Thank God for divine security!

The next portion of this biblical assurance takes us to a higher level of divine security, which I call "divine safety".

So Israel will live in safety;
Jacob will dwell secure
in a land of grain and new wine,
where the heavens drop dew.
Blessed are you, Israel!
Who is like you,
a people saved by the LORD?

He is your shield and helper

and your glorious sword.

Your enemies will cower before you,

and you will tread on their heights. – Deuteronomy 33:28–29.

Governments everywhere rightly place a major emphasis on safety, because everybody needs to feel safe where ever they live in this world. That's why safety has become a major concern. As I often wonder, were it not for an urgent need for safety, would so many wars have taken place? Probably not. With that in mind, you can understand why our God promises us everlasting "divine safety." And honestly, that's the only safety we can depend on one hundred percent. Also, that's the only safety that's free of charge. There is no price tag attached to it, because Jesus-Christ has already paid the price through his death on the cross. All we have to do to receive the inheritance of "divine safety" is to accept it and claim it by faith through the merit of Jesus-Christ. It is a permanent, eternal inheritance. The good news is that it will always be available because God is the one who makes it available for you. – *1 Peter 1:4; Hebrews 9:15.*

People who believe they can acquire enough security in the world to remain safe and secure have been misguided. If your life is not under God's umbrella of "divine security," you are simply not safe. Notice what David said:

> *The Lord watches over you—*
>
> *the Lord is your shade at your right hand;*
>
> *the sun will not harm you by day,*
>
> *nor the moon by night.*
>
> *The Lord will keep you from all harm—*
>
> *he will watch over your life;*
>
> *the Lord will watch over your coming and going*
>
> *both now and forevermore.* – Psalm 121: 5–8.

I think the sentiment of all believers should sense their profound need for "divine security." Jesus rightly said: *Without me, you can do nothing.* – John 15:5.

Through sincere devotion and communion with God, David assimilated very well the notion of divine security. *LORD, you alone are my portion and my cup; you make my lot secure.*

The boundary lines have fallen for me in pleasant places; surely I have a delightful inheritance. – Psalm 16:5–6.

When our hearts are fully opened to the treasures of God's kingdom, we'll be able to realize that He created them for our inheritance.

God's inheritance is past, present, and future. This means that God's blessings have been made available in the past, in the present, and they will continue to be available in the future. His divine inheritance of safety is everlasting. Read the following scriptures as you reflect on the availability of God's blessings through his inheritance.

The inheritance is a manifestation of grace and love. The psalmist explained how God, being his Shepherd, provides everything he needs in order for him to be secure within the confines of the inheritance,

The LORD is my shepherd, I lack nothing.

He makes me lie down in green pastures,

he leads me beside quiet waters,

he refreshes my soul.

He guides me along the right paths for his name's sake.

Even though I walk through the darkest valley,

I will fear no evil, for you are with me;

your rod and your staff, they comfort me.

You prepare a table before me

in the presence of my enemies.

You anoint my head with oil; my cup overflows.

6 Surely your goodness and love will follow me

all the days of my life,

and I will dwell in the house of the LORD forever. – Psalm 23:1–6.

The inheritance is accessible. Train yourself to be godly. For physical training is of some value, but godliness has value for all things, holding promise for both the present life and the life to come. This is a trustworthy saying that deserves full acceptance. That is why we labor and strive, because we have put our hope in the living God, who is the Savior of all people, and especially of those who believe. – *1 Timothy 4:8-10*.

The inheritance is the manifestation of strength and endurance for life's challenges.

Have you not heard? The LORD is the everlasting God, the Creator of the ends of the earth. He will not grow tired or weary, and his understanding no one can fathom. He gives strength to the weary and increases the power of the weak. Even youths grow tired and weary, and young men stumble and fall; but those who hope in the LORD will renew their strength. They will soar on wings like eagles; they will run and not grow weary, they will walk and not be faint. – *Isaiah 40:28-31*.

The inheritance brings peace of mind and heart for you and your descendants This is what the LORD says: Your Redeemer, the Holy One of Israel:

"I am the LORD your God, who teaches you what is best for you, who directs you in the way you should go. If only you had paid attention to my commands, your peace would have been like a river, your well-being like the waves of the sea. Your descendants would have been like the sand, your children like its numberless grains; their name would never be blotted out nor destroyed from before me. – Isaiah 48:17–19.

Bible reading exercise

By faith the walls of Jericho fell, after the army had marched around them for seven days.

By faith the prostitute Rahab, because she welcomed the spies, was not killed with those who were disobedient. And what more shall I say? I do not have time to tell about Gideon, Barak, Samson and Jephthah, about David and Samuel and the prophets, who through faith conquered kingdoms, administered justice, and gained what was promised; who shut the mouths of lions, quenched the fury of the flames, and escaped the edge of the sword; whose weakness was turned to strength; and who became powerful in battle and routed foreign armies. Women received back their dead, raised to life again. There were others who were tortured, refusing to be released so that they might gain an even better resurrection.

The writer of the book of Hebrews intended to open our spiritual eyes to what we may be able to accomplish through faith and action. As you read the entire chapter it becomes obvious that all the men and women of God who were able to fly high in their achievements, had two things in common: faith and spiritual maturity.

Bible reading exercise for faith and spiritual maturity

Today, I invite you to meditate on the following biblical verses where the apostle reminds you about the nature of your fight which is spiritual. He admonishes you to be equipped with spiritual weapons in order to fight in this kind of battle. Meditate on the following scripture as you practice praying for faith and spiritual maturity, or as you embark on this most important trip toward claiming your inheritance:

Finally, be strong in the Lord and in his mighty power. Put on the full armor of God, so that you can take your stand against the devil's schemes. For our struggle is not against flesh and blood, but against the rulers, against the authorities, against the powers of this dark world and against the spiritual forces of evil in the heavenly realms. Therefore put on the full armor of God, so that when the day of evil comes, you may be able to stand your ground, and after you have done everything, to stand. Stand firm then, with the belt of truth buckled around your waist, with the breastplate of righteousness in place, and with your feet fitted with the readiness that comes from the gospel of peace. In addition to all this, take up the shield of faith, with which you can extinguish all the flaming arrows of the evil one. Take the helmet of salvation and the sword of the Spirit, which is the word of God.

And pray in the Spirit on all occasions with all kinds of prayers and requests.

With this in mind, be alert and always keep on praying for all the Lord's people. Pray also for me, that whenever I speak, words may be given me so that I will fearlessly make known the mystery of the gospel, for which I am an ambassador in chains. Pray that I may declare it fearlessly, as I should.

The inheritance provides permanent access to the blessings of the kingdom even while you are still here on Earth. Some believers are waiting to make it to heaven before they can acquire God's inheritance. This is really a misconception, because the kingdom of God is really past, present, and future; it is everlasting. Just the same as His inheritance is past, present, and future. It's been accessible to believers of all ages and generations. That's why when you become a kingdom-minded believer, you will begin to enjoy the blessings of God's kingdom even before you make it to heaven. - *Hebrews 4:15-16.*

The inheritance allows you to have a solid anchor in the spirit. You can be steadfast and sure even when the billows roll; even when the entire world is confused and discouraged, you can have the certitude of God's blessings and miraculous intervention.

The inheritance allows you to count on your fortune while others count on their misfortune. When you understand that God's inheritance is your inheritance, you start enumerating the wealth of God's treasures in spite of your present situations. You know what God has reserved in His storehouse for you. By faith you can count on His infinite blessings.

The wisdom of God is granted to us through spiritual maturity. This makes it possible for us to understand and practice the deepest revelations of God. At this level of spiritual maturity, you are able to see opportunities that others don't see because you are functioning in the Spirit, not in the flesh. The spirit reveals things to you that the flesh cannot reveal. You are also able to accept God's manifestation in your life before it even takes place. You can even claim your victory by faith before it takes place.

Notice what Paul said: *We do, however, speak a message of wisdom among the mature, but not the wisdom of this age or of the rulers of this age, who are coming to nothing. No, we declare God's wisdom, a mystery that has been hidden and that God destined for our glory before time began. None of the rulers of this age understood it, for if they had, they would not have crucified the Lord of glory. However, as it is written:*

> *"What no eye has seen,*
>
> *what no ear has heard,*
>
> *and what no human mind has conceived*
>
> *the things God has prepared for those who love him—*
>
> *these are the things God has revealed to us by his Spirit.*

– 1 Corinthians 2:6–9.

As you open your heart and mind to be the recipient of God's inheritance, beware of any personal resistance on your part that may stop the flow of your blessings. As I have already discussed in this chapter, God will not bestow on you any blessings that you are against.

You must focus your thoughts and action on the abundance that you expect to receive from the Lord in order to have access to it. Do not waste your spiritual, mental, and physical energy on anything that blocks your inheritance from manifesting in your life. You will be able to experience miracles that you would never even imagine possible. Thus, keep your eyes focused on your inheritance as you are determined to claim it by faith.

Points worth special attention

- Open up your heart for abundance through God's inheritance. He will not bless you with anything that you willfully resist.
- Train your mind daily to depend on divine security and safety. If you depend too much on secular security and safety, you will be disappointed. True and everlasting security and safety can only be experienced through the manifestation of God's power.
- Envision yourself as a guest sitting around the golden table at God's banquet. This will remind you how special you are to Him.
- Take a moment every day to praise God for His goodness. You will experience it in everything that you do while you put your faith to work.

Notes

_____

_____

_____

_____

_____

_____

_____

Chapter 13:

Plugging into Life's Energy Outlet

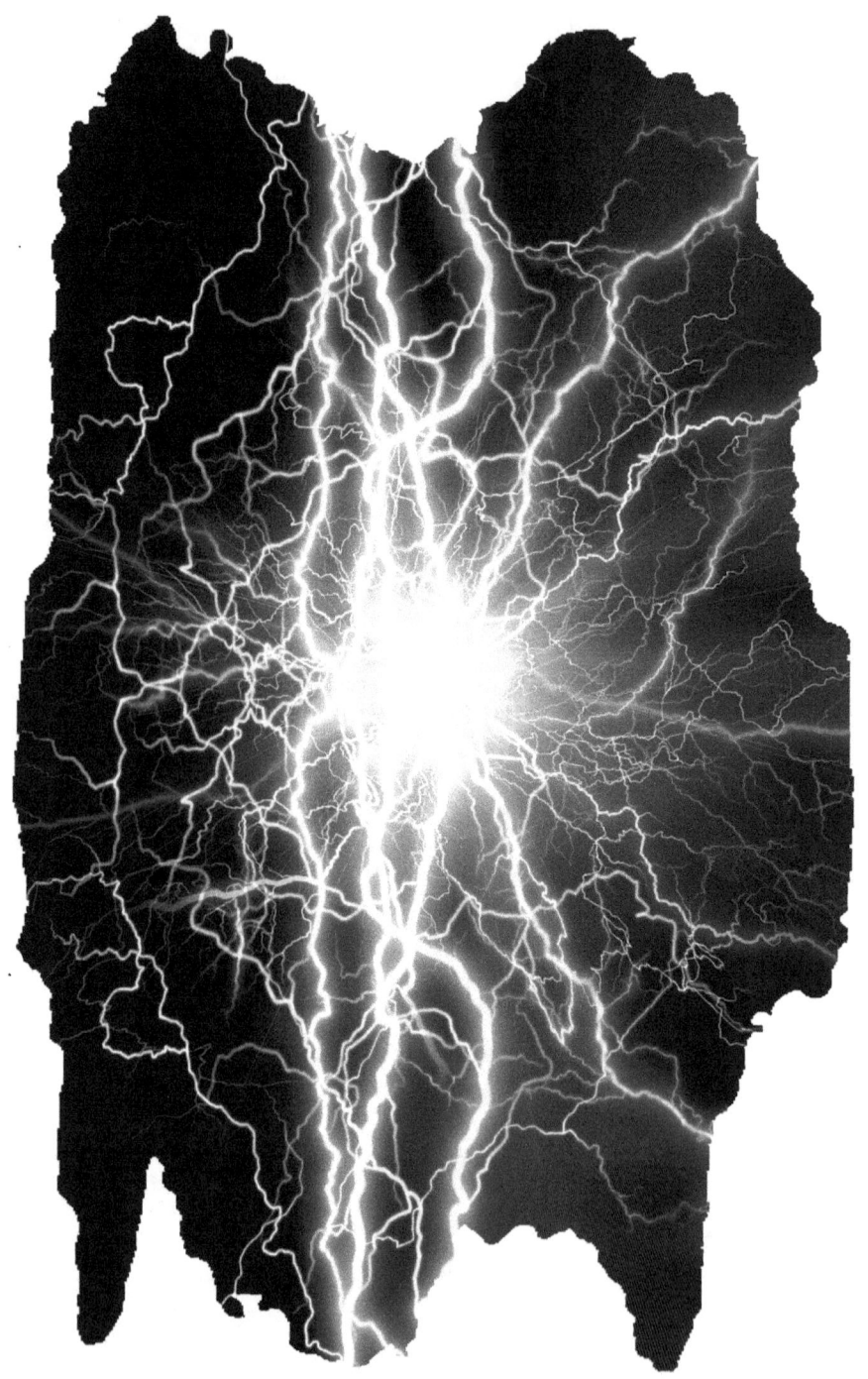

It is interesting to discover where an electrical outlet gets its power from. It ultimately comes from a power generating station operated by the electric utility co. There, a generator is turned on by water from a dam (hydroelectric) or by steam from coal or oil, or sometimes a nuclear reactor. The generating station might be many miles away.

A very tiny bit of electricity is produced from the sun (photovoltaic), and by wind generators too.

Have you seen the huge metal towers with cables up on top? These transmission lines are how the electricity gets from the generating station into the city. The transmission lines go to substations, where the voltage is transformed down to a lower value, then distributed by wires on smaller poles into neighborhoods. There, it is transformed once more into a lower voltage, the proper value for your outlets. This is done by transformers. Sometimes they are round metal cans up on poles, sometimes they are square metal boxes in a front yard or alley. Finally, the electricity comes from the transformer to your house. There may be a cable overhead from a pole to the house, or sometimes the cable is buried underground.

Once the electricity is at the house, wires in the attic and walls carry it to the outlet itself. Whew! What a journey!

Have you ever wondered why some prayers are able to remove mountains while others are not? The difference lies in the fact that in order for our prayers to remove the mountains in our lives, we must acquire the power to plug ourselves into God's energy out. As a result, His power is made accessible to us whenever we are in need of it. That's when our prayers become legitimate and wonder-working, and we become willing and ready to cooperate with God. In this case, He allows our strength to back up our supplications as His power flows through us.

The power will not flow through us until we willingly and earnestly seek to connect to God through constant communion and supplications. That's one of the lessons God intended to teach to His people when Moses had to hold up his hands to God in order to receive power to conquer his enemies:

As long as Moses held up his hands, the Israelites were winning, but whenever he lowered his hands, the Amalekites were winning. When Moses' hands grew tired, they took a stone and put it under him and he sat on it. Aaron and Hur held his hands up—one on one side, one on the other—so that his hands remained steady till sunset. So Joshua overcame the Amalekite army with the sword.

Plugging into God's energy outlet means to raise our faith

to His level. It also means to step up by faith just as Moses had to raise his staff and stretch out his hand over the Red sea so that the Israelites could go through the sea on dry ground. Immediately after Moses has done that, God miraculously divided the waters for the deliverance of His people:

Then the Lord said to Moses, "Why are you crying out to me? Tell the Israelites to move on. Raise your staff and stretch out your hand over the sea to divide the water so that the Israelites can go through the sea on dry ground. I will harden the hearts of the Egyptians so that they will go in after them. And I will gain glory through Pharaoh and all his army, through his chariots and his horsemen. The Egyptians will know that I am the Lord when I gain glory through Pharaoh, his chariots and his horsemen."

Then the angel of God, who had been traveling in front of Israel's army, withdrew and went behind them. The pillar of cloud also moved from in front and stood behind them, coming between the armies of Egypt and Israel. Throughout the night the cloud brought darkness to the one side and light to the other side; so neither went near the other all night long.

Then Moses stretched out his hand over the sea, and all that night the Lord drove the sea back with a strong east wind and turned it into dry land. The waters were divided, and the Israelites went through the sea on dry ground, with a wall of water on their right and on their left.

The Egyptians pursued them, and all Pharaoh's horses and chariots and horsemen followed them into the sea. During the last watch of the night the Lord looked down from the pillar of fire and cloud at the Egyptian army and threw it into confusion. He jammed the wheels of their chariots so that they had difficulty driving. And the Egyptians said, "Let's get away from the Israelites! The Lord is fighting for them against Egypt."

Elisha's experience is very similar to that of Moses. It teaches us to keep our spiritual eyes open in order to experience the wonder-working power of God while enjoying our relationship with Him daily. That's when our prayers are able to remove mountains.

When the servant of the man of God got up and went out early the next morning, an army with horses and chariots had surrounded the city. "Oh no, my lord! What shall we do?" the servant asked.

"Don't be afraid," the prophet answered. "Those who are with us are more than those who are with them."

And Elisha prayed, "Open his eyes, Lord, so that he may see." Then the Lord opened the servant's eyes, and he looked and saw the hills full of horses and chariots of fire all around Elisha.

As the enemy came down toward him, Elisha prayed to theLord, "Strike this army with blindness." So he struck them with blindness, as Elisha had asked.

Elisha's experience gives us the secret to prayers that remove mountains. They are not just a repetition of words. They are the heartfelt expressions of believers with a clear vision of what God is able to do when we trust Him. The vision of Elisha's servant was so limited that Elisha had to ask God to open his spiritual eyes so he could see. After his spiritual eyes were opened, he could witness the manifestation of God's power. We can easily be afraid of our obstacles and challenges when we have a limited vision of what the Lord can do. In order for us to fully experience the manifestation of God's power, we must plug our prayers into the right energy outlet which gets its energy from heaven's power generating station (The throne of God).

Prayer warriors fly high because they plug into God's spiritual energy outlet. Prayer warriors are those believers who have been able to find God's true energy outlet by tracing it from the word of God. His word is the only way to make sure that you plug your prayers into His energy outlet, which is faith. Here's what the writer of the book of Hebrews said:

Now faith is confidence in what we hope for and assurance about what we do not see. This is what the ancients were commended for. By faith we understand that the universe was formed at God's command, so that what is seen was not made out of what was visible. – Hebrews 11:1–3.

In this case, faith is God's energy outlet, and prayer is the extension cord. Once your extension cord is plugged into the right energy outlet, you really don't have anything to worry about. Your miracles are already in place.

Christians should realize that with faith in God, and persistent prayer, nothing is impossible. As someone stated once, "More things are wrought through faith and prayer than by any other means." Before we go any further, I want to take a few moments to trace a small portion of the miraculous history of prayer in the bible. This will allow us to understand the means through which God operates His miracles.

Through Elijah's faith and prayer, an entire nation returned to God after witnessing the manifestation of His power:

At the time of sacrifice, the prophet Elijah stepped forward and prayed: "Lord, the God of Abraham, Isaac and Israel, let it be known today that you are God in Israel and that I am your servant and have done all these things at your command. Answer me, Lord, answer me, so these people will know that you, Lord, are God, and that you are turning their hearts back again." Then the fire of the Lord fell and burned up the sacrifice, the wood, the stones and the soil, and also licked up the water in the trench. When all the people saw this, they fell prostrate and cried, "The Lord—he is God! The Lord—he is God!"

It's impossible for the human mind to comprehend what God can do when our extension cord is plugged into His energy outlet. In the Scriptures quoted above, you were able to depict how God operates from the energy outlet and through the extension cord to manifest His power and glory through you.

> "More things are wrought through faith and prayer than by any other means."

First, without connection, there is no energy. That's why believers should connect their extension cord every single day into God's energy outlet in order to have access to God's miraculous power supply.

Secondly, without faith and prayer, even if the energy outlet is available, we'll not be able to benefit from it. Thirdly, nothing will be done until you willfully and purposefully connect your extension cord into God's energy outlet.

Fourthly, nothing is impossible through Jesus-Christ: *I can do all things through Christ who strengthens me.* – Philippians 4:13.

Our childlike faith moves God, not our complaints. The kind of faith that moves God is often called childlike faith. It is really the secret behind the miracles that He performs in the lives of His children. Childlike faith simply means a faith that is doubt-free. Jesus, in His teachings on faith and prayer, placed a major emphasis on it because it is the kind of faith that can move mountains through the manifestation of the Holy Spirit. Note the words of Christ in the following scriptural passages. – *Matthew 17:20, 21; 21:22.*

Childlike faith causes us to trust God even when we don't see any signs of deliverance in our situations. We just know and know that the Lord will make a way. He does not need any means to make a way. He is in the way making business. He alone is able and capable of making a way out of no way. With God, all things are possible. Pray for God to grant you a childlike faith. It's a major secret of the power of prayer.

Biblical examples of childlike faith

The woman with the issue of blood. *And a woman was there who had been subject to bleeding for twelve years. She had suffered* *a great deal under the care of many doctors and had spent all she had, yet instead of getting better she grew worse. When she heard about Jesus, she came up behind him in the crowd and touched his cloak, because she thought, "If I just touch his clothes, I will be healed." Immediately her bleeding stopped and she felt in her body that she was freed from her suffering. At once Jesus realized that power had gone out from him. He turned around in the crowd and asked, "Who touched my clothes?" "You see the people crowding against you," his disciples answered, "and yet you can ask, 'Who touched me?' " But Jesus kept looking around to see who had done it. Then the woman, knowing what had happened to her, came and fell at his feet and, trembling with fear, told him the whole truth. He said to her, "Daughter, your faith has healed you. Go in peace and be freed from your suffering." – Mark 5:25–34.*

The blind man of Jericho. *When he heard that it was Jesus of Nazareth, he began to shout, "Jesus, Son of David, have mercy on me!" Many rebuked him and told him to be quiet, but he shouted all the more, "Son of David, have mercy on me!" Jesus stopped and said, "Call him." So they called to the blind man, "Cheer up! On your feet! He's calling you." Throwing his cloak aside, he jumped to his feet and came to Jesus. "What do you want me to do for you?" Jesus asked him. The blind man said, "Rabbi, I want to see." "Go," said*

Jesus, "your faith has healed you." Immediately he received his sight and followed Jesus along the road. – Mark 10:47–52.

Those two miracle recipients did not have the same needs; they did not have the same prayer requests; what they had in common was their childlike faith. As we practice our childlike faith in God, we will touch God in marvelous ways. He will perform for us miracles that are far beyond our expectations. He will do more than what we pray for in order for His name to be glorified.

Points worth special attention

- Plug into God's energy outlet daily and allow God's spiritual energy to flow through you.
- Pray every day for God to open your spiritual eyes in order for you to witness the manifestation of His power and glory.
- Expect positive changes in your life. As a channel freely open to God's favors. I can assure you that positive changes will take place in just about every aspect of your life: Spiritually, mentally, physically, financially and otherwise.
- Pray daily for God to instill in you a childlike faith that trusts Him one-hundred percent for the answers you need to achieve your goals.

Conclusion: Completing the Journey

As you purposefully embark on this upward journey toward having a Solution Oriented Mind, I strongly advise you to elevate your faith to a much higher level through the infinite power of the Holy Spirit. That's the principal secret of believers who accomplish miraculous things in life. What sets them apart is that they have the faith and tenacity to request and accept a double portion of the Holy Spirit. The Bible speaks of Zerubabel, who had a great task ahead. As the governor of the Jewish province at that time, he lacked the military strength to move forward. The task was at a standstill, causing the returning Jews to be afraid. Their fear was based primarily on the fact that they were not in great numbers and that they were poor; but, their enemy who was harassing them was strong and very active. In order to encourage the hearts of His people, God assured them they needed to depend on the unfailing power of the Holy Spirit in order to be unstoppable.

Here's what He said to them: *Not by might, nor by power, but by my Spirit, says the Lord of Hosts.* – Zechariah 4:6.

I would encourage you to write this verse someplace where

you can always have access to it in order to remind yourself constantly, that everything is possible through the power of the Holy Spirit. You will not be able to do it on your own merit and strength, but with the Holy Spirit empowering you, everything is possible.

Your greatest challenges will pave the way for your greatest blessings. Notice the great inspiration displayed in the experience of Gideon toward the deliverance of the people of God. While Gideon thought he didn't have enough men to fight the battle, God told him he had too many. God didn't want him to think that he won the battle because he had enough human support. He didn't want Gideon and his army to boast about their human strength. That's why he reduced Gideon's army to a very insignificant number in comparison with the enemy's army. God reduced Gideon's army from thirty-two-thousand to only three hundred.

The LORD said to Gideon: *You have too many men. I cannot deliver Midian into their hands, or Israel would boast against me, "My own strength has saved me." Now announce to the army, "Anyone who trembles with fear may turn back and leave Mount Gilead." So twenty-two thousand men left, while ten thousand remained.*

But the LORD said to Gideon, "There are still too many men. Take them down to the water, and I will thin them out for you there. If I say, 'This one shall go with you,' he shall go; but if I say, 'This one shall not go with you,' he shall not go.'

So Gideon took the men down to the water. There the LORD told him: Separate those who lap the water with their tongues as a dog laps from those who kneel down to drink. Three hundred of them drank from cupped hands, lapping like dogs. All the rest got down on their knees to drink.

The LORD said to Gideon: With the three hundred men that lapped I will save you and give the Midianites into your hands. Let all the others go home. So Gideon sent the rest of the Israelites home but kept the three hundred, who took over the provisions and trumpets of the others.

What you may learn from Gideon's experience is that God's ways are different from ours. That's why we must always seek the guidance of the Holy Spirit so that we may learn to know His ways, His likes, and His dislikes. We may do so by communing with Him through prayer, meditation, and the study of His word. It is really amazing how those who frequent the prayer room often become very acquainted with God's ways. In essence, prayer is the gateway to the knowledge of God which, in itself, is life everlasting.

The Holy Spirit helps us to know and understand God's wisdom and majesty. When we know God and understand His wisdom and majesty, we realize that it is impossible for us to lean on our own strength. Even if we assemble all the strongest people on Earth together, it still would not suffice to guarantee our victory when we face life's challenges. No matter how strong we think we are, we need the power of the Holy Spirit to empower us as we walk in the light of God's word.

Get ready to enjoy God's fountain of life as you walk in the light. You have learned, thus far, through the pages of this book, that you cannot separate life and light because they function together in the context of God's manifestation of power in the life of a believer. They are two of the most remarkable and infinite manifestations of the all-pervading and omnipotent power in God's universe. They are the pivotal points that affect and control all aspects of creation in the universe. In fact, the universe could not exist without them. God granted us access to life and light in order to reveal to us a glimpse of his power and majesty.

Notice what David said: *For with thee is the fountain of life; in thy light shall we see light.* – Psalm 36:9.

As you come to the realization that God is the source of all being, you will digest the concept that anything connected to that source is unstoppable.

Having explained the role of the Holy Spirit in God's manifestation of power, I now want to take a spiritual trip with you through the role and merits of Jesus Christ in all the positive changes that will be taking place in your life. My purpose here is to introduce Jesus Christ as the only true way to *The Solution Oriented Mind*. Without a strong spiritual relationship with Him, we would never be able to experience a spiritual rebirth.

> *Oh, the depth of the riches*
> *of the wisdom and knowledge of God!*
> *How unsearchable his judgments,*
> *and his paths beyond tracing out!*
> *"Who has known the mind of the Lord?*
> *Or who has been his counselor?"*
> *"Who has ever given to God,*
> *that God should repay them?"*
> *For from him and through him and for him are all things.*
> *To him be the glory forever! Amen.*
> *– Romans 11:33–36.*
> *For us there is but one God, the Father,*
> *from whom all things came and for whom we live;*
> *and there is but one Lord, Jesus Christ,*

through whom all things came and through whom we live.

– 1 Corinthians 8:6.

Notice that when speaking of His relationship to His father, Jesus said: *If God were your father, you would love me, for God is the source of my being, and from Him I come.* – John 8:42.

That was Jesus' way of saying that He and His father constitute that divine source which generates life and light, causing the universe to exist. That's what we all need to depend on for *The Solution Oriented Mind*.

Jesus Christ is also the source of life and light. As the second person of the Godhead He is co-creator with God the father, and God the Holy Spirit. He is also the only true highway to heaven and The Solution Oriented Mind. It is vital for you to understand what He represents to you as an integral part of the principal source of life in the universe.

Here's what John said: *In the beginning was the Word, and the Word was with God, and the Word was God. He was with God in the beginning. Through him all things were made; without him nothing was made that has been made. In him was life, and that life was the light of all mankind. The light shines in the darkness, and the darkness has not overcome it.* John 1:1-4.

The Solution Oriented Mind has been made available to

you through the grace and merits of Jesus-Christ. In the past, God spoke to our ancestors through the prophets at many times and in various ways, but in these last days he has spoken to us by his Son, whom he appointed heir of all things, and through whom also he made the universe. The Son is the radiance of God's glory and the exact representation of his being, sustaining all things by his powerful word. After he had provided purification for sins, he sat down at the right hand of the Majesty in heaven. Hebrews 1: 1-4

What does that do for us? Through Him we now have full access to the throne of grace. We no longer have to depend on our own strength in order to make it. We just have to establish a solid relationship with Him by faith, and the power of the kingdom will be made available to us. I know for some, this may appear too easy. What you need to understand is that, because He himself is the principal source of power, by connecting to Him, that power can be made manifest in us.

Believers who connect to Jesus Christ through prayer and meditation will inevitably experience His power in everything they do. I know you're reading this because you aspire after a positive change in your life, or because you want to improve your relationship with the Lord, but the good news is, with that relationship comes the power to rise higher in all your endeavors.

That power becomes automatic because of your communion with Him and your adherence to the principles of the kingdom of God. Christians all over the world can testify to this. If you are not a believer, I strongly and urgently encourage you to become one. This would be the most important decision of your life as it would pave the way for a new you with an upward mentality. However, if you are already a believer in Jesus Christ, I encourage you to continue putting your faith in action in order to experience a higher dimension of His power and saving grace.

Notice what Paul had to say concerning the supremacy of Jesus Christ as our principal source of power for change: *The Son is the image of the invisible God, the firstborn over all creation. For in him all things were created: things in heaven and on earth, visible and invisible, whether thrones or powers or rulers or authorities; all things have been created through him and for him. He is before all things, and in him all things hold together.* – Colossians 1:15–17.

It is nearly impossible to fully explain how, through Jesus Christ, God the father has made everything available to us by the power of the Holy Spirit. The three constitute a divine trio creating for us things that are over and beyond what we never imagine.

Here's what Jesus said: *Very truly I tell you, the Son can do nothing by himself; he can do only what he sees his Father doing, because whatever the Father does the Son also does. For the Father loves the Son and shows him all he does. Yes, and he will show him even greater works than these, so that you will be amazed. For just as the Father raises the dead and gives them life, even so the Son gives life to whom he is pleased to give it. Moreover, the Father judges no one, but has entrusted all judgment to the Son, that all may honor the Son just as they honor the Father. Whoever does not honor the Son does not honor the Father, who sent him.* – John 5:19-23.

I am the light of the world. Whoever follows me will never walk in darkness, but will have the light of life. Whoever follows me will never walk in darkness. – John 8:12.

These are some of the most powerful promises of Jesus Christ in a world where darkness seems to keep humanity in blindness and confusion, losing their sense of orientation. As followers, you have the sacred and blessed privilege of walking in the light. As an eagle, you can fly higher and higher with clear vision of your destination. You just need to constantly remind yourself, even while experiencing your greatest challenges, that you can't miss your target if you keep your eyes focused on Christ.

Notice what He said: *I am the way and the truth and the life. No one comes to the Father except through me. If you really know me, you will know[b] my Father as well. From now on, you do know him and have seen him. John 14:6-7*

Through Jesus Christ, *The Solution Oriented Mind* will help you make the most out of your life's failures and disappointments while you are here on Earth, as He paves the way for you to inherit eternal life.

Now that you are reminded of the role that Jesus Christ plays in your manifestation of power, think about what life really is, and make up your mind to praise Him for life as you wake up every single day. If we only knew what life really is, we would thank God every day for the miraculous and mysterious gift of life. Every time we open our eyes and see the light, we would magnify His name. We would wake up every day with the determination to make the most out of every minute. We would understand that there is no such thing as life without God. God is the true source of life. In other words, He is life. As much as secular humanistic theories are trying to separate life from God, they will never be able to.

It's impossible to dissociate life from its principle source. You now have the advantage of making your dreams come true by tapping into that limitless source on a daily basis. That power is mysterious and miraculous. You and I will never be able to explain it. We just have to simply enjoy it. Of course, you cannot enjoy what you don't accept. You have to earnestly and honestly pray for it, claim it, and accept it by faith. May God grant you *The Solution Oriented Mind.*

www.ingramcontent.com/pod-product-compliance
Lightning Source LLC
Chambersburg PA
CBHW061758110426
42742CB00012BB/1921